How Teachers Learn Technology Best

by Jamie McKenzie

FNO Press
Bellingham, Washington
http://fnopress.com

FNO Press   http://fnopress.com

This work contains articles previously published in a number of journals and publications.

"Lifting the Siege" first appeared in the April, 1998 issue of **The School Administrator**.

"Grazing the Net" first appeared in **From Now On** and then again in the September, 1998 issue of **Phi Delta Kappan**.

"The Information Literate School Community" first appeared in the March, 1999 issue of **Connected Classroom**.

"Secrets of Success," "The Software Trap," "Gauging Return," "Creating Learning Cultures," "Invention as Learning," "Online Learning," "Coaching for a Change," "Creating a Vanguard," "Reaching the Reluctants," "Planning for Success," "Study Groups," "Work Place Visits" and "Picking Up the Tab" all appeared as columns in **eSchool News**.

"Learning Digitally" and "Strategic Teaching" were first published in **From Now On**.

ISBN 0-9674078-1-8
Printed in the USA.

This collection is dedicated to my wife, Gretchen, my favorite teacher and best friend, whose love, guidance and support were a major inspiration to me throughout the period these essays and articles were created.

About the author . . .

Jamie McKenzie is the Editor of **From Now On - The Educational Technology Journal**, a Web-based **ZINE** published since 1991. In this journal he has argued for information literate schools. More than 25 per cent of his 19,000+ subscribers live in countries outside of the United States such as Australia, New Zealand, Sweden, Malaysia and Singapore.

From 1993-1997, Jamie was the Director of Libraries, Media and Technology for the Bellingham (WA) Public Schools, a district of 18 schools and 10,000 students which was fully networked with 2000 desktops all tied to the Internet in 1994/95. He has now moved on to support technology planning and professional development for districts across North America as well as Australia and New Zealand.

A graduate of Yale with an MA from Columbia and Ed.D. from Rutgers, Jamie has been a middle school teacher of English and social studies, an assistant principal, an elementary principal, assistant superintendent in Princeton (NJ) and superintendent of two districts on the East coast. He also taught four-year-olds in Sunday school.

Jamie has published and spoken extensively on the introduction of new technologies to schools. In recent times he has paid particular attention to information technologies and how they might transform classrooms and schools to support student centered, engaged learning.

A full resume listing publication credits and a detailed career history is available online at http://fno.org/resume.html.

Introduction

During the final decade of the twentieth century, schools in many countries spent huge sums running cables and buying computers to connect classrooms to the Internet. For this investment to pay dividends - to dramatically strengthen the skills with which students read, write and learn about their world - schools must offset this spending on equipment with two critical elements: 1) a clear focus upon program goals and 2) the provision of extensive professional development opportunities for all teachers.

Now that many schools are placing networked computers in all classrooms, we should be asking which strategies are most likely to convert these new technologies into tools that are welcomed and embraced by all classroom teachers. We should be asking how we can maximize the benefits for all of our students.

This book is about the search for successful strategies and the answers found during two decades of trying to integrate electronic technologies into classrooms.

The first section of the book is devoted to questions of purpose. We have evidence that many teachers are reluctant to use new technologies until we can show them how these tools will help them to deliver on their primary missions (teaching math, reading, science, etc.)

We know that more teachers will agree to learn and use new technologies if they can expect to see improved student performance as a result of their efforts. Many teachers are skeptical about the rush to network schools and think of this effort as one more in a long series of bandwagons that have passed across the educational landscape during the past three decades.

Introduction

The second section of the book outlines an approach to the design of adult learning experiences intended to reach a broad spectrum of teachers. During the first two decades of introducing new technologies, we have focused too narrowly upon software and pioneering teachers. We have done much training but devoted little time to adult learning concepts. We have failed to reach the late adopting and reluctant teachers who make up the majority of our faculties.

We can do much better.

The next decade may bring a dramatic shift as schools and teachers place greater emphasis upon thinking, questioning and information skills, recognizing that networks make possible what the Australians have called "information literate school communities." With the right program goals and matching professional development opportunities, we can create a generation of young people capable of wrestling thoughtfully and skillfully with difficult questions, problems and decisions.

Contents

Part One

Why Network

Chapter 1 - Lifting the Siege

Many schools are finding out with considerable pain that it is not enough to install an expensive network tying all classrooms to the Internet. It is not enough to place a laptop in the hands of each student. After all that money and all that planning, some schools still find themselves suffering from the **screensaver disease**.

We are talking about the educational equivalent of **Red Ink** . . . the observable failure of schools to actually use their network or computers to any meaningful extent because they are not seen as part of the school's primary mission and teachers are ill prepared to integrate them into their classroom activities.

After two decades of effort and billions of dollars, computers and new technologies remain peripheral (read "tangential" or "irrelevant") to life in the typical American classroom. Except for a hardy group of pioneers who have shown what is possible, the bulk of our teachers lack the support, the resources, or the motivation to bring these intruders into the classroom core. These technologies remain for the most part "outside the walls of the city" like the Greek armies surrounding Troy.

We do not need a Trojan Horse to end this siege. New technologies will be welcomed and used daily by the vast majority of teachers when schools pay attention to a few simple lessons we have learned in districts that have been successful.

- Make learning goals very clear
- Identify the classroom opportunities
- Provide extended funding and commitment
- Emphasize robust staff development, adult learning and the creation of a supportive culture
- Combine rich information with powerful tools
- Match rigorous program assessment to learning goals and student outcomes

1. Make learning goals very clear

In all too many cases, technology plans are silent when it comes to student learning or they wax eloquent on lofty goals which relate to the millennium, the workplace and the society at large - goals which translate poorly into daily classroom realities. Until classroom teachers are shown how new technologies can improve the way students learn and think in social studies, science and math class, they are unlikely to sit up, take notice and make significant use of these new tools.

Successful districts make use of planning guides such as **Plugging In**, an excellent document from the North Central Regional Educational Lab that highlights **Engaged Learning** as the purpose for technology:

Engaged learners are:
- responsible for their own learning
- energized by learning
- strategic
- collaborative

Engaged Learning challenges teams of students to employ information technologies to investigate authentic problems which parallel curriculum questions and topics. In a similar vein, **Information Power**, a publication developed by the nation's librarians, suggests that our goal must be to show students how to solve problems and make decisions.

Lifting the Siege

Technology is not an end in itself. It is merely the highway or the car or the airplane which takes you where you want to go.

Successful districts put **student learning** at the forefront of their planning, and then they design a technology project which combines the best of staff development practices with curriculum development and network installation.

2. Identify the classroom opportunities

Teachers are most likely to embrace technologies if they can see the connection between their work (covering and exploring the curriculum) and the tools.

> "How does this help me teach social studies or writing?" they might reasonably ask.

The best strategy is to write technology expectations into the curriculum guides. Every curriculum document should identify learning experiences and strategies which require the use of new technologies.

For example, the language arts curriculum must state clearly that students in second grade right up through the end of high school will compose 10-15 papers annually using word processing software in combination with rich electronic information sources.

The curriculum guide outlines the requirement that these writing exercises be done in concert with the principles of "writing as process" which takes students through stages from pre-writing to final draft - all on the computer.

In a similar manner, the social studies and science curriculum should name the occasions for analysis of data, global e-mail partnerships and investigations using electronic information.

Why are we doing this? How we do reading, writing, 'rithmetic and reasoning is all changing with the arrival of the new information technologies. Good schools step out in front of these changes and ask how to build a curriculum which prepares students for the future they will inherit.

3. Provide extended funding and commitment

All too often the focus of technology planning is limited to the selection, purchasing and installation of hardware and infrastructure. One sees far too little attention to what must happen prior to installation and what must follow.

We must think of this venture as a five year journey at least. The technology plan should focus on cultivating and developing as well as installing.

Sometimes it works to use a gardening metaphor. Those who fail to cultivate and fertilize the soil prior to planting rarely achieve a harvest worth mentioning. Those who fail to weed, maintain and develop the garden, once planted, are likely to see their plantings languishing or failing to thrive.

Cultivating the Soil

In the case of technology, the "soil" is the community of learners and teachers who will be expected to use these powerful new tools. It makes no sense to wait until all of the equipment arrives to begin the all important "human resource development" outlined in the next section. Those districts that increase "technology readiness" by investing in a vanguard or cadre of talented people will reap the greatest benefits when the bulk of the installation takes place.

Without this cultivation stage, districts are likely to fall victim to a technology-driven design. They may not know how to use these technologies to support the curriculum, and the districts will probably turn to outsiders who know little about classroom learning to design, install and manage the networks.

Technology-driven design is shaped by the interests and perspectives of network engineers and business people who may not have the vaguest clue about learning, student research models or the design of information systems to support students and classrooms.

4

Lifting the Siege

Technology-driven design often results in the highest percentage of disuse and screensavers. The network operates smoothly but delivers nothing worth a student's time. The resulting configuration of computers and the offering of information services is often irrelevant to life in schools.

An example of education-lite technology design would be the decision to place three networked computers in every classroom of a district. This model does not work for teachers or students but it sure makes installation and network planning simple.

Those who have tried creating "technology powerful classrooms" find that you need one computer for every 3-4 children in a self-contained elementary classroom and one for every 2-3 students in secondary classes which switch every 40 minutes. They have also found that it is a waste of resources to put so many computers in the room of a teacher who intends to lecture all day.

The technology-driven design ignores these classroom realities and places cable and computers everywhere.

Ongoing Funding, Resource Development and Commitment

Few districts project the true cost of keeping the newly installed network operating over the post-installment decade. In fact, most plans are silent on "replacement" and make no financial plan to address the 36 month life span of the modern computer. This failure can leave districts sitting with slow-moving dinosaurs wearing the Emperor's New Clothes.

Thanks to the planned obsolescence of computer hardware and software companies (Shenk, 1997), schools may only count on three years' of reasonably efficient use of any computer. Soon the new software slows performance so dramatically that staff and students are spending a third of their seat time just waiting and watching. Each district must plan ahead for this phenomenon.

Two other issues require <u>sustained</u> commitment. The first of these is the **development of effective information resources** to be offered over the network. A primary purpose of a network is the delivery of information that richly supports the curriculum.

This challenge is a constantly evolving one requiring a substantial investment of time and money as the information products (on-line periodical collections such as *Electric Library*, *EBSCO* and *ProQuest*) are in their infancy and require careful testing before purchase. They also require an enormous amount of time and labor to install on a network. Some people think the job is done when the computers are installed and linked. Installation is only the first quarter of the game if you intend to provide a robust network that supports the learning goals of the schools.

The second major issue requiring sustained commitment is the **technical staff support to extend and develop the contents of the network.** Few districts hire enough technicians to service and support the ongoing development of the **network content.** Each new information product and each new piece of software may require hundreds of hours of installation time, but most districts have so few technicians that the installation of these products can be delayed for months or simply ignored.

Once a district spends millions on a network, it should hire enough technicians to make sure the network operates in an efficient and robust manner optimizing return on investment.

4. Emphasize robust staff development, adult learning and the creation of a supportive culture

Staff development is the most effective insurance policy against the **screensaver disease** identified earlier. The best way to encourage teachers to embrace these technologies is to give them personal learning experiences which win them over to the worthwhile classroom activities which are now possible.

For too long we have failed to provide adult learning that shows how to employ the technologies to explore topics from social studies, science, language arts, or math. The technology classes have all too often been mere applications classes . . . *Cool Things You Can Do with*

Excel or *Advanced Desktop Publishing* taught by well meaning colleagues who may know the application but not know how one might use *Excel* in social studies class to crunch *Census* data.

This challenge is not about **training**. It is about **learning**. If we expect teachers to turn around and use technologies daily with students they need to discover personally the power of the new technologies when combined with rich information. We also need to provide more informal support structures such as mentors, coaches and "just in time help" that often do more to promote risk taking and growth than formal class offerings.

5. Combine rich information with powerful tools

The best way to enlist a much larger percentage of teachers in the use of technology is to offer them a combination of rich information and powerful tools. Those who have held out for decades against fads and bandwagon drill-and-kill software can be won over by good information actually relevant to the curriculum.

If we engage teachers in researching authentic problems such as treatment options for Alzheimer's Disease or cancer, the response can be very positive. Once teachers see what we mean by **Information Power,** they will often embrace what they once rejected.

6. Match rigorous program assessment to learning goals and student outcomes

Assessment is a powerful tool for program revision and change. In the case of Bellingham (WA), the continued use of instruments such as the *Mankato Scale* to measure learning by staff and students since 1995 has made a major contribution to the design of the program and the creation of staff development opportunities at the building level. Originally created by the Mankato (MN) Schools, this self-reporting survey has been revised to match Bellingham's evolving program goals. Copies are available for downloading at http://www.bham.wednet.edu/assess2.htm

Each June, teachers apply rubrics to match their performance levels. Here is one example from the **Mankato Scale**:

____ Level 1- I do not use Netscape, nor can I identify any uses or features it might have which would benefit the way I work.

____ Level 2 - I can start up Netscape and use district World Wide Web menus to find basic information on the Internet, but I spend little time doing so.

____ Level 3 - I am able to make profitable use of Web searching software as well as lists of Internet resources to explore educational resources.

____ Level 4 - I can create my own HTML pages and hot-lists of resources. I have shown my students how to mine the information resources available on the Internet as well as other networked information sources.

As a second part of the assessment strategy, the district developed performance tasks requiring teams of students to solve problems with new technologies. This component led to major changes when it revealed that students were more skilled at pushing buttons that they were at communicating, analyzing data and solving problems cooperatively in teams.

Unfortunately, the failure to assess the results of technology investments continues in most places today. Ignoring assessment is like driving a car or flying a plane blindfolded. If we do not measure what students can do with these new technologies, we are likely to keep on doing tomorrow what we did yesterday even if that strategy is a waste of time.

Assessment provides a reality check. It affords us a chance to switch directions and steer the program towards the destination we chose when we set out.

7. Combining the elements

We can end the siege, effectively bringing new technologies into the core of the regular classroom program if we combine all of the elements listed above in a concerted, systematic approach. This combination will require balanced, prolonged funding and a sense of strategy. Those districts who persist in putting all of their technology eggs in the hardware basket are likely to wake up with Humpty Dumpty screen savers. Those who invest in human resource development, rich information and authentic assessment to accompany their hardware purchases will bestow the gift of **Information Power** upon staff and students alike.

Online Resources

http://fno.org/techtopten.html
Enjoy the ten sites I have selected as the **Technology Top Ten**. All of these sites provide significant resources to guide a school or district forward in the use of technology to support engaged learning and student centered classrooms.

Chapter 2 - Learning Digitally

The arrival of networks and electronic information could bring about a major improvement in the ability of students to read, write and reason. Schools and homes now have tools and resources available that might transform learning into something more enticing, more valuable and more widespread.

Unfortunately, these wonders will not happen simply because we buy and install networks. They will not occur because we place laptops on children's laps. Learning digitally will only transform schools and student performance if we make wise program decisions, invest mightily in professional development and emphasize strategic teaching as outlined in the preceding chapter.

Disclaimer . . .
Books, librarians and libraries are still vital!

Even though digital resources and networking may eventually transform how students think, communicate and solve problems, it must be noted up front that we shall still require good books, librarians and libraries for the foreseeable future to balance electronic sources and help us find our way.

We have seen that information literacy is a critically important element in the successful introduction of networked information. We need educators with a strong sense of information science to help every student and every teacher acquire good navigating and interpretive skills.

There is entirely too much talk about replacing librarians, books and libraries with the Internet. This is folly. Madness. Intellectual disarmament. The free Internet, while vast in size, is plagued with weaknesses when it comes to disorganization, reliability and quality.

Even though it might be madness, there are hundreds of schools across North America that have furloughed the librarian and replaced them with computer teachers and the Internet. This is a dangerous trend that makes absolutely no sense for an Age of Information. At the same time that students need radically stronger information skills, some schools and districts are dismantling the programs that might equip them.

How may learning change with the addition of rich information and powerful tools?

1. We can expect to see tremendous growth of independence along with an increase in the range, the depth, the complexity and the originality of the thinking and production. Students will learn to make up their minds free of the "spoon fed" simplicities and homilies that have dominated many classrooms for too long.

Range

For some categories such as news, networked information will vastly extend the reach of anyone asking questions or exploring issues. We are no longer limited to the printed pages that arrive at our doors in the morning or the periodicals ordered by our local and university libraries.

Provided we have the right telecommunications linkages, we can check out what folks are thinking this morning in Stockholm, Auckland, Beruit and Lima without leaving our bedrooms or our classrooms and without waiting for the mail to be delivered. Networks can help our students to escape a narrow, local, provincial or ethnocentric perspective. They support a more global view.

This amplification of range will only occur if there is a thirst for knowledge and a willingness to seek out the foreign and the unusual. Just because a window or a door is open doesn't mean that folks will look outside.

Some school districts have found that e-mail, which carries with it the potential for global exchanges, is often used for primarily local communication. It does not automatically turn young people into global citizens. Others are too scared to permit e-mail at all.

Depth

While I have written at length about the "Age of Glib" and the McDisneySoft communications empire that oversimplifies, entertainerizes and infantalizes much of the new information available electronically, the advent of networked information could support deeper explorations. Along with mainstream sources that tend to oversimplify, students might also take advantage of extensive archives that offer primary sources as rich as an untapped vein of coal.

Interested in turn-of-the-century American life? Visit and explore the 30,000 images available at the Library of Congress.
(http://lcweb.loc.gov)

Ironically, the Internet sometimes distorts truth until it tastes like processed cheese, but it can also offer up mammoth helpings of undiluted, raw data that is free of contamination and interpretation. First hand accounts, diaries, census data, art collections and photographic portfolios are examples of electronic resources which surpass anything we have known in the past. To access archives of such depth and scale we had to travel to universities, libraries, museums or government archives. Today they lie a mouseclick away over the network.

Complexity

The cabbage patch has been transformed into Monet's garden.

Prior information technologies - like the textbook -selected, summarized, distilled and simplified the world for young folks. Much of the world was portrayed in "white bread" simplicity. While the McDisneySoft empire maintains its commitment to this traditional simplification of reality, the newer technologies offer up a dazzling array of contrasting, conflicting, colliding perspectives and possibilities. We go from telescope to kaleidoscope.

As with all the potentials mentioned previously, complexity is simultaneously subverted and supported by the Web. One can find diversity, complexity and spice if one wishes. One can also find burnt white toast.

Originality

Fresh perspectives and wide open windows to the seething new electronic bazaar of ideas could promote fresh Paris open air market thinking unlike anything we have witnessed in the past.

Innovation and originality thrive on the free flow of ideas and experiences. At the same time, much of the new information and the electronic media suffer from clip art banality and a template sense of style. Just as much of the world has been GAPped by the mass marketers, the news wires and McDisneySoft empire undermine creativity with their unrelenting drive toward standardization and "ready made" ideas.

The Web allows mavericks, clowns, heretics, poets and fools to publish their work without bowing before the editors, sages, and elders who have so long dominated the flow of ideas. This is a decidedly mixed blessing, of course, because it means the startling insight and bold dash of color may be submerged in a flood of mediocre and disappointing offerings.

As with the other potentials we can ascribe to digital learning, the prospects for a surge of creativity and originality will require some promotion and catering. None of this will happen automatically. While some idea generation will thrive spontaneously like a virulent virus, much of the good will be offset by countervailing viruses spawned by mass marketing and mass media. Clip art, templates, and user friendly short cuts will undermine some of the best prospects.

2. We can also expect to see a dramatic shift in the nature of community along with the modes and the nodes of communication.

Kevin Kelly's provocative book, **New Rules for the New Economy** takes us well beyond current notions of information and knowledge as he explores the impact of networks on the ways that people communicate, exchange ideas, build community and do business.

Few schools have even approached the challenge of preparing young people with the skills they will need to manage the tasks and the media of the next decade. Even the most forward thinking of the many studies projecting workforce needs into the next century fall short of identifying these realities.

According to Kelly, basic assumptions of the past decade will cease to operate and influence will pass to those who know how to "grow networks." The old rules centered on capturing segments, markets, technologies and domains. They rewarded preservation and conservation. Entrepreneurs sought ownership of market turf. They built corporate castles, moats and draw bridges that shackled and bound them to behaviors that could not keep pace with the kinds of change that accompanies vast, breeding networks.

The new rules require release, extension, and propagation. Instead of holding on, one lets go. Rather than clutch, one relaxes one's grip and releases one's hold, sending great value out across the network in ways that will come back around like a boomerang hurled into the Australian Outback.

Kelly explains how we are moving from a resource-based economy to a connected knowledge economy. Change, he explains, is radically different under these new conditions.

> Change comes in various wavelengths. There are changes
> in the game, changes in the rules of the game, and changes
> in how the rules are changed.
> Kelly, Page 114

Kelly differentiates between two categories of change: selective FLUX and CHURN. CHURN he sees as change without much intention, purpose, value or direction. Selective FLUX, on the other hand, he sees as productive, developmental and evolutionary.

How do we teach our students to distinguish between the countless waves and surges? How do we prepare them to start paddling in time to catch and then ride the more promising waves? How do help them learn to let go, cut away, shift direction and take advantage of backwash, surge or undertow?

Many of the Internet's pioneering school efforts have centered on communities of learners exchanging data, ideas and inventions across state or national boundaries. In the best of these projects, the results have been consistent with Kelly's vision as students from two countries (the USA and Sweden) may develop a Web site to explore media literacy. In quite a few, however, the projects showed little payoff for the global community being constructed around the task at hand.

Much depends on the elders.

According to some of the promises and the marketing missives, you might expect to see schools and learning transformed with the mere laying of cable, as if infrastructure by itself could infuse teachers and students with skill, wisdom and judgment simply by increasing connectivity.

It just isn't true. Impressive student outcomes might result from an investment in networked information and communications, but only if the elders do their part.

1. Support

The underlying notion behind this networking is that students must learn to explore and communicate for themselves. While this hardly sounds like a revolutionary point of view, there is little student exploration and problem-solving in many classrooms. For networks to make a difference, teachers must embrace and support student learning and the value of exploration. Saddled with enormous pressures to cover thick curriculum guides and produce performance on increasingly difficult state tests, many teachers find it difficult to carve out space in the schedule for such time consuming student investigations.

So long as a majority of teachers may value teaching above learning, we are unlikely to see dramatic changes in student performance as a result of networks.

2. Structure

The mythology surrounding new technologies promotes surprisingly haphazard and irresponsible experiments that often create such poor results that critics and skeptics feel entirely justified in doubting the value of the enterprise and the new resources. Those who send their students down the hall to "surf" the Net often find that they return with hundreds of pages of questionable findings. It turns out that successful searching and efficient electronic investigations must rest upon a carefully developed, structured foundation of information literacy skills that would include solid questioning, prospecting, translating and inventive abilities.

Despite the marketing hype, we are unlikely to see improved reading, writing and reasoning because of new technologies unless we combine them with "strategic teaching" - the thoughtful application of best practices to the new tools. Without such "strategic teaching," according to some studies, the quality of student writing may actually decline as a result of computers. Sadly, the tendency to ignore or underfund professional development means that powerful new tools are used in ways that deflate their impact and potential. Professional development is probably the most important ingredient in the technology mix. Its absence, like the absence of yeast in bread dough, may produce nothing but flat and disappointing results.

Best practice now suggests the need to equip students with skills and structures before they drive the electronic highway. Surf boards no longer suffice. Models like WebQuest help direct student efforts around organizing questions, tasks and concepts so that time is spent productively and students wrestle with significant issues.

3. Guidance

If students are engaged in learning, then teachers do much less teaching. They act more like coaches, helping to shape student efforts through a mixture of modeling and suggesting. This is a very difficult transition for many teachers who have spent their lives knowing the answers. They were respected for their expertise and their knowledge. Suddenly they are expected to take a back seat and let students find and make their own answers. Many of the questions and problems (c.g., "What policy should the USA or New Zealand or Australia or Japan or Taiwan have toward China?") may be unanswerable in any final or finite sense. Problem-based learning is messier than the old smokestack model that required that teachers spout answers while students commit them to memory.

Guidance involves substantial silence and abstention. Tempting as it may be to take mouse or problem in hand and clear away the problem, more learning occurs when the teacher remains in the background requiring the learner to take responsibility for the mouse and the solution. This kind of learning is about "giving away" the skills and the power. The best indication of success is when the teacher has equipped the students to fly from the nest with considerable independence.

Far too little attention has been devoted to the creation of professional development models that would help teachers grow these "guide on the side" skills and strategies. Most professional development for technology still centers around how to use the tools, the software applications and the resources. There is little focus on strategic teaching or guidance . . . little focus on "unteaching" or the "unteachable moment."

Successful teachers of this method are sometimes a blur through the room. At other times, they are rooted alongside a pair of students digging deeply.

There is no sure fire formula or recipe for success with this method. It requires a continual diagnostic/prescriptive approach, as the teacher roams, browses and monitors. High on the list of skills is the ability to "size up" the progress and the process being used by each student or student team. It is important to keep moving and looking. While some teachers may expect students to call them over or ask for help, it is unlikely that all students will know when they are in need of help or coaching.

An important aspect of this kind of teaching is the goal of requiring students to become tool makers and strategy builders. The teacher holds back from handing over tools and strategies and solutions.

"What's the best way to do this?" they coach. "What's worked for you in the past? How can you build on that?"

Basic to the method is the goal of building student autonomy and independence. We cannot reach that goal as teachers unless we are willing to relinquish control. Success depends upon a substantial amount of letting go.

4. Encouragement

As with most creative enterprises, this kind of learning can be frustrating and discouraging. Good teachers know how to provide timely emotional support as well as skills and structures. Exploration of controversial issues and confounding problems is often disheartening. The worst moments may precede the best moments, as illumination often emerges from frustration and blockage. Good teachers also know when to stay back, allowing the student thinker to experience the fullness of intellectual inquiry. It helps if the teacher prepares students for these emotional dimensions by acquainting them with the stages of creative inquiry so they may manage much of their own emotional distress as part of the process.

5. Deliverance

While the book and the movie **Deliverance** connote a terrifying ride down a river, digital learning, in its best sense, is about a different kind of deliverance. We are talking about setting students free with a solid skill base to do their own thinking. We will equip them with the ability to break free of undue reliance upon pundits, middle men and middle women. We expect them to face the toughest questions of their lives with resilience, self reliance and competence.

The Value of Rubrics

For many decades we have paid too little attention to standards clearly expressed at the beginning of a project or assignment. Recent attention to ongoing assessment and rubrics has made it much easier for students to understand what we expect from them and to shape their efforts toward those ends.

Rubrics are a fine example of the adult structures that can help deliver a return on our technology investment, but some teachers are finding that students can learn to develop their own rubrics. They report that students care more about the standards when they have a voice in their creation.

One of the most distressing disappointments of the technology bandwagon is the proliferation of flashy but intellectually weak multimedia presentations that utilize every transition and special effect possible but offer less content, less thought and less value than old fashioned "go find out about" encyclopedia research projects. We are seeing too much of what I have called the "New Plagiarism" dressed up in clip art and fancy special effects.

In working with a national multimedia contest recently, I offered several rubrics meant to "raise the bar" and require both originality and style.

Originality

We need to clarify the expectation that students will produce some new thought and new ideas, not merely rehash the ideas, contributions and thoughts of others. What counts is the inventiveness of these young thinkers, researchers and problem-solvers. They should know up front that they will develop original concepts, solutions and possibilities. We warn against the currently trendy preference in many

places for packaging over content. At the same time we guard against
"content is king" approach that is a time-honored school tradition.

Rubric for Originality & Inventiveness

1 The work is a meager collection or rehash of other
people's ideas, products, images and inventions.
There is no evidence of new thought.

2 The work is an extensive collection and rehash of
other people's ideas, products, images and inventions. There is no evidence of new thought or inventiveness.

3 The product shows evidence of originality and
inventiveness. While based on an extensive collection of other people's ideas, products, images and
inventions, the work extends beyond that collection
to offer new insights.

4 The product shows impressive evidence of
originality and inventiveness. The majority of the
content is fresh, original and inventive.

Style

One of our goals should be the development of judicious and
elegant use of design principles. It is not just whether graphics match
the text. It is whether they are PLEASING to the eye. Sometimes
"less is more." There are issues of balance and proportion. If our goal
is to teach persuasive communication, then we must ask if the glitter,
the movement and the graphical elements actually CONTRIBUTE to
UNDERSTANDING. In many quarters, it is enough to be COOL! The
challenge is to teach young designers not to be distracted from idea
generation and communication by the temptations of Jumping Jack
Flash.

Rubric for Style

1 Exaggerated emphasis upon graphics and special effects weakens the message and interferes with the communication of content and ideas.

2 Graphical and multimedia elements accompany content but there is little sign of mutual reinforcement. There is no attention paid to visual design criteria such as balance, proportion, harmony and restraint. There is some tendency toward hodge podge.

3 Design elements and content combine effectively to deliver a high impact message with the graphics and the words reinforcing each other.

4 The combination of multimedia elements with words and ideas takes communication and persuasion to a very high level, superior to what could be accomplished with either alone. The mixture brings about synergy and dramatic effects that reach the intended audience with style, pizazzz and elegance.

Quality

If we expect to see dramatic improvements in student reading, writing and reasoning, the issue of quality becomes central. Rubrics offer one of the best ways to clarify our expectations in ways that will produce the results we seek. Silence on those same quality issues only helps to maintain the status quo.

Learning Digitally

The Importance of Scaffolding

Well intended progressive efforts of the past have foundered and floundered because, among other reasons, there was not enough structure to maintain quality. Many of the more current approaches have emphasized scaffolding of various kinds as a strategy to enhance student performance and production.

Scaffolding allows considerable leeway while maintaining parameters and limits.

Developmental stages

Recognizing that younger children may not be able to handle the unstructured new information landscape as well as older, more highly skilled students, we would recommend a greater level of direction, guidance and structure for them.

1. Concentric rings

We would expect that all students might begin their research with high quality resources such as books and encyclopedias and then move outward to explore increasingly diverse and disorganized sources once they have established a foundation of understanding and knowledge.

2. Look before you leap

We encourage students to begin with authoritative lists of good sources rather than wading through monstrous lists of search engine hits. Some commercial products like *Encyclopaedia Britannica* and *Encarta* offer Internet links that are intended to reduce the need for searching and sifting. User interfaces like these can speed students toward relevant, authoritative and reliable information that might otherwise remain obscured in the vast information heaps of the Internet.

Learning Digitally

High Standards

Many states have clarified expectations for student learning that are quite well aligned with the elements of digital learning outlined earlier. Illinois, for example, has standards for Language Arts that are right on target. Students are expected to demonstrate strength in 1) problem-solving, 2) communicating, 3) using technology to access information, process ideas and communicate results, and 4) working in teams.

Scenario One - A Question of Courage . . .

What does digital learning look like?

You enter a middle school classroom and find that students are engaged in half a dozen different activities. Half the students are clustered in pairs and trios around computer monitors. They are trying to decide which of a dozen pictures does a better job of representing courage. More importantly, they are writing papers summarizing their findings. They are substantiating their interpretations, demonstrating visual literacy.

Try your hand at this activity with a partner. Go to the **Thinker**, the online exhibit of the San Francisco Fine Arts Museum that shares more than 70,000 images. (http://www.thinker.org)

Once you find the imagebase and read the copyright notice, do a search for "courage" and decide which three pictures deserve your attention. Copy and paste these images into your word processing program and then write a paper that compares and contrasts the three pictures with regard to their portrayal of courage. Which one does the best job? Why?

Digital resources are especially well suited to exercises that challenge a student to make and defend choices, building a case by gathering and explaining evidence. Archives are so extensive they support a wide variety of activities and increase the chance that students will be able to work on issues that matter to them.

Learning Digitally

Scenario Two - All the News that's fit . . .

What does digital learning look like?

You enter a high school classroom and find that students are exploring news coverage of a hot international conflict on the dozen laptops that they have brought to class and plugged into the network docking stations installed in all six corners and along all six walls of their irregularly shaped room. They have found sufficient electrical support along with networked information.

The teacher has located several Web sites that offer up links to hundreds of newspapers from around the world. Students are busily comparing foreign coverage with that of the US press. **CNN, USA Today**, the **New York Times**, and the **Washington Post** are compared with **Le Monde, Figaro**, etc.

The reach of student exploration far exceeds anything possible a few years back. Far from being captive of the McDisneySoft empire, these students can see strands of bias and national trends in coverage. They can further distinguish threads of conflict within individual nations as newspapers on the right report the news one way while their left wing counterparts see and report the facts differently.

Scenario Three - The New Neighborhood

Young people may emerge from this century with a new sense of neighborhood . . . a far more global perspective that includes friends and like-minded thinkers from all around the world.

They will sometimes find they have more in common with people from other countries than they do with people who live just down the road.

With the right introduction to global communication and with the permission to use e-mail (which is often blocked by schools), our students can begin preparing for an adult work life that will rely more and more upon team invention across electronic networks.

There are already some outstanding examples of this phenomenon and this possibility. The ThinkQuest contest has promoted invention by students across international boundaries.

Students from Sweden combined with students from Hawaii, for example, to build a Web site devoted to media awareness. There are dozens of other examples of excellent student projects at this site. (http://thinkquest.org/library/17067.html)

Judi Harris of the University of Texas has gathered together a master list of online projects that engage students as teams in various kinds of learning and problem-solving. The possibilities seem endless. (http://www.ed.uiuc.edu/Activity-Structures/web-activity-structures.html)

During the past ten years, many people have discovered the pleasure of building friendships and working relationships across state and international boundary lines.

In the 1920s, writers and artists felt they had to cross the ocean to spend time with other artists and thinkers in Paris. Today, they can trade ideas and invent good things while separated by thousands of miles. Thanks to e-mail and various forms of conferencing, we can build electronic communities around shared interests, issues and goals.

Despite the amazing potential of this new medium, some schools have been remarkably resistant to students having e-mail at all. The press has done such a job of scaring people about the risks of e-mail, that many school leaders have taken the route of blocking student access altogether, an astoundingly wasteful approach to the use of a very expensive network.

Barriers and Obstacles
Why is the journey so difficult?

Even though we pour billions of dollars into new technologies, there is no credible evidence yet that these vast expenditures have resulted in the kinds of benefits outlined as possibilities above.

Why is this so? Aside from the failure to fund professional development and adequately staff the new networks, it seems that schools have been frozen between tradition and chaos. The proponents of new technologies are so often guilty of exaggerated, simplistic claims and hype that they are easily dismissed by the skeptics and doubters who eagerly point out the many failures and misfires that so often accompany these new installations.

A failure to clarify learning goals lies at the heart of this conundrum. Schools have a long history of simultaneously resisting and embracing bandwagons in such a way that no real change seems to materialize despite all the sound and fury. Networking has fallen prey to some of the same "virtual change" characteristics. We have all the outward accoutrements without much of the substance. Too many schools are networking for networking's sake. They uncritically do technology as if it were a goal in itself.

Resistance and inertia cannot be eliminated simply by cabling a school. Stasis, a lack of blood flow, cannot be cured by installing new equipment. Stasis is a cultural phenomenon. Organizational development is the cure. Not hardware. Unfortunately, technology proponents rarely seem to understand the steps required to energize a staff and equip them with the instructional repertoire required to take full advantage of digital learning tools.

The Road Ahead

We stand on the brink of disaster and opportunity. Those more foolish and wasteful early efforts to introduce networking will soon inspire an acrid trail of newspaper articles and news programs that will "out" the scandals and failures of the past five years. Taxpayers will demand results. The thoughtless, fad-driven wiring of schools will slow down and be replaced by much more purposeful ventures as parents realize that the mere wiring of schools does not improve, modernize or reform schools, that wiring in itself does not contribute to the quality of education.

When parents see that their children's use of these expensive networks is often heavily shackled by fearful network and school administrators, they will begin demanding a better return on investment. When they see the quality of their children's research and their access to reliable information decline as they spend hundreds of hours wandering across the vast wasteland of the Internet, they will ask why crowns and dollars and yen have been diverted from libraries and books, from roof projects and art projects, to fund this new information delivery system.

In the next two years we will see many schools commit themselves to clear learning goals, robust professional development programs and assessment models with a focus on stronger reading, writing and reasoning. Time is running out for those who fail to convert technology dollars into real gains, real opportunities and the exciting possibilities outlined in this article.

Schools that commit to digital learning and the qualities associated with information literate school communities will find that their investment pays handsome dividends.

The Results

Imagine the benefits if Australia, New Zealand, Canada, Sweden, Chile, and the United States all managed to dramatically increase the capacity of their young people to make up their own minds, work in teams, invent new possibilities, communicate effectively and make a substantial contribution to their communities.

The health and the well being of democratic societies depend upon developing such capacities. Without them, our basic values are at risk.

Chapter 3 - Strategic Teaching

Strategic teaching requires thoughtful choices. An effective teacher has a toolkit of strategies that can dramatically modify student performance when the choice of tool fits the situation and the individual student. The best teachers are great at "sizing up" a student's patterns in order to figure out how to jump start improvement.

Intervention for Growth

Timely intervention is required in order to boost performance. Left undisturbed, most students routinely apply what they already know to tasks. But it is these routines - like flat tires - that often need changing.

Wrong routines lead to wrong answers . . .

Answering comprehension questions, the student may apply the following routine to the task:

"The main idea is always found in the first sentence."

The effective teacher steps in at the right time - intervenes - to bring about a burst of newly directed activity. The new direction radically improves performance. The student steps out of the bog, exchanges hip boots for running shoes, sprouts wings, sprints at top speed and finally lifts off the ground. The line graph tilts up and to the right. The score is higher. Life improves.

In a society that opens and closes doors based upon test performance, strategic teaching creates more opportunities and richer choices. It confounds predictions based upon background. It supports upward mobility and provokes the blooming of talent. Strategic teaching frees potential from the grip of tradition, low expectations and apathy.

Strategic Teaching

Four Types of Intervention

Not all teacher interventions are appropriate, helpful or timely. There are four interventions that hold the great promise, however, especially when they are applied in a customized fashion as a combination to match the student's profile.

1. Adds to the student toolkit as needed

As students pass through life and school, adults often hand them tools and show them new ways of doing things. Unfortunately, the timing of these adult gifts may not coincide with student need or readiness. Rather than grasping the gift and putting it to good use, the student may drop it on the way out the classroom door or may ignore its presence entirely. Later when the mental saw or drill might be most helpful, the student stands helpless and ill-prepared . . .

"What am I supposed to do with this mess?" they complain.

Just as rain may fall so heavily in a single hour that the ground cannot absorb it fast enough to prevent flooding and run-off, schools may bombard students with skills before they are ready to absorb and apply them.

One antidote to "skill run-off" is the teaching of skills in the context of real problems so that students see their value. But strategic teachers take this responsibility a step further. In addition to ongoing efforts to expand student toolkits in a developmental manner, they frequently monitor the toolkit of each student to see which tools have "slipped through the cracks." They intervene to provide each individual student with enough support to make essential tools a permanent part of the toolkit. They time intervention and support to match the challenges at hand.

2. Untangles wrong thinking

When students fail to perform, select wrong answers and end up in the wrong place at the wrong time, their difficulties may often be traced to tangled thinking and wrong rules. They approach the problem or challenge with the wrong operating procedures and the wrong strategies. Given more practice on the same kinds of problems, they are apt to keep right on with the tangled thinking and the wrong rules.

Effective teachers ask students to reveal the patterns of their thinking . . .

"How did you come up with that answer?" they ask.

This diagnostic process is central to the intervention process. If teachers do not take the time to ask, it is unlikely that they will be able to match interventions to individual students. Remedial programs become parking lots instead of repair shops.

Once the teacher knows how the student is approaching the problem, the teacher may help to untangle the thinking and may suggest some better strategies to apply in the future.

Looking over one student's shoulder at a huge list of irrelevant "hits" on a search engine, it becomes apparent that the student is not applying good search strategies.

The teacher asks, "How can you target your search to focus on just the right information?"

The student shrugs, not understanding.

The teacher then launches into a brief mini lesson in "Telling Questions" and Boolean Logic so the student will search more skillfully. Even though she knows this student has been taught these skills previously at the opening of the unit, it is clear that the skills never took root. She hopes that their value will prove more obvious in context.

Even as she leads the student through the mini lesson, the teacher is making a mental note to include the student in some small group tutorials on search strategies with other students who have been showing a need for follow-up sessions.

3. Empowers independent problem-solving

The effective teacher rarely picks up the student's problem and rarely touches the student's mouse or track pad. The emphasis is firmly placed on developing independence and autonomy.

Noting that a pair of students seem stuck on their research path, spinning wheels without going any place, the teacher stands close by, listens in to the conversation and actually abstains from intervention until 15-20 minutes later, knowing that some frustration is basic to the creative process. He knows that he must not jump in too quickly, thereby robbing the student team of authentic learning. He is aware that synthesis often requires some incubation and struggle. Content that the students are wrestling with the challenge in an earnest manner, he moves along to monitor the progress of other groups.

"Mr. Frederico? How can I get some decent information on crime?"

A student is tugging at his elbow insistently. He could simply tell the student to visit the Bureau of Justice. He could supply the URL. He could share some statistics already downloaded. But he wants this student to gain independence.

"Remember the strategy we discussed, **Going to the Source?** How do you think that might help here"

The student frowns at first, a bit irritated that the request has been turned back around. "You mean, like, figure out where it might be? Who might have the information?"

Mr. Frederico nods. "Sure. Who do you think has the best information on crime?"

The student's frown deepens. "The cops?"

Mr. Frederico smiles. "Keep going," he says. "In fact, I'd like you to go back to your laptop and make a list of six possible sources and then test them out on the Net. See which one proves most helpful."

The student is not entirely happy with this exchange. Instead of finding a short cut to his information, he has been asked to hone his search skills. If the teacher had handed over the answer instead of returning the responsibility to the student, he would be supporting a dependency relationship that would deprive the student of authentic learning.

Strategic Teaching

4. Encourages invention of new tools & skills

Independent problem-solving often requires the invention of new tools and strategies. Sometimes it simply requires new ways of using old tools. One way or another, students must learn to modify their toolkit, making new tools and bending the old ones to the new tasks at hand.

"This isn't fair! They haven't taught me how to do that."

In times of rapid change, the unexpected is expected, the unthinkable is common, and the anomaly is commonplace. Students will need a "change ethic" in order to manage the inconsistencies and surprises that are so typical of life and learning in the Age of Information.

A change ethic involves a spirit of welcoming change and surprise along with a toolkit of strategies to manage those surprises. Effective teachers work on developing both the spirit and the toolkit, showing students how inventiveness pays off in the world they are inheriting. See Chapter on Inventiveness in **Parenting for an Age of Information.** http://fno.org/parenting/inventing1.html

Networked schools must place a premium on students inventing new ways of doing things because so many encounters with technology involve learning new rules, new procedures and new operating procedures. Because many sites are "interactive," the visitor actually invents the visit by combining various features and exercising certain options.

Search engine sites are a good example of this phenomenon. They are so chock-full of special features, that each visitor might search in very different ways.

HotBot's Super Search (http://www.hotbot.com/) is a prime example.

When typing search words into the search box, the student may select from a menu of seven choices directing how HotBot should treat those words . . .

1. all the words

2. any of the words
3. exact phrase
4. the page title
5. the person
6. links to this URL
7. Boolean search

Unfortunately, few users seem to use or understand the power of these choices.

The list of choices goes much further . . .

1. You can limit the choice to a specific language.
2. You can limit the choice to a range of dates.
3. You can limit the choice to a specific location or domain.
4. You can limit the choice to pages containing specific words or not containing certain words and phrases.
5. You can enable "word stemming."
6. You can ask for as many as 100 or as few as 10 "hits."
7. You can specify page depth.
8. You can specify that pages must contain certain media types.

Each time the visitor conducts a search, the page offers a chance to invent a unique combination of words and features to optimize results.

For one search, features 1, 4, 7 and 8 might combine for the best outcomes. For a different search, features 2, 3 and 7 might be best. Using the right syntax, the searcher combines words, logic and features into a rich "search stew."

If the searcher relies upon nothing more than the simple search box, considerable power is lost. The results are more likely to be information swamp than information stew.

Strategic Teaching

The effective teacher shows students these search features and models good searching. But more importantly, the effective teacher makes clear that inventive use of the features is required to match the special characteristics of each search for information. This is not a situation where recipes will suffice. Students must learn that effective searching is something like cooking from scratch without relying upon a cookbook.

A Professional Development Strategy

Teachers can learn to broaden and deepen their repertoire to include more strategic teaching strategies. Bruce Joyce has published extensively on the value of teachers mastering multiple models.

Too little attention has been devoted to the challenge of equipping teachers with such strategies. In the rush to wire schools, the focus has been overwhelmingly upon the hardware and the electronic infrastructure.

Professional development for strategic teaching would combine five elements . . .

1. Reviewing Techniques

Whenever we hope to encourage more mindful teaching with consistent and deliberate practice of challenging and rewarding strategies, we might begin by creating a clear picture in each teacher's mind of the techniques we hope they will employ. We need to offer models of good practice and invite teachers to add these techniques to their own repertoire.

In the case of strategic teaching, many good teachers already employ some of the interventions outlined above, and they will quickly recognize their value. These same teachers are likely to view the other interventions with interest and take a serious look at how they might prove beneficial.

The first stage in this professional development strategy, then, might be called an "awareness" stage that is meant to acquaint teachers with the menu of opportunities. The goal is to spark interest while outlining possibilities.

2. Critiquing Video Models

The next stage "puts flesh on the bones" of the methods introduced in the first stage by engaging teachers in critiquing videotaped classroom sessions. Some of these will be outstanding examples of strategic teaching. Others might be the antithesis (or opposite) of good practice. The goal is to engage teachers while sharpening their appreciation of key elements in successful teaching.

3. Practicing Techniques

We have research evidence that suggests the value of teachers testing difficult strategies with small groups prior to attempting their use in regular classroom settings. Micro-teaching is a method that has been used with success for several decades now as a way to acquire and hone new skills. After each session, the teacher may review a videotape of the lesson to consider what worked, what aspects fell short and what needs to be done to enhance technique.

4. Learning from Feedback

Some teachers welcome feedback from a trusted colleague or suggestions from a skilled expert. Others are quite reluctant to participate in such programs. One way to handle this difference in style is to offer feedback as an option to those who request it. While some teachers can add to their repertoire without any outside feedback, the act of teaching requires such intense focus that it is difficult to notice all that is happening in a classroom and a second pair of eyes can deepen our understanding of our impact.

5. Enjoying Support

The work of Joyce, Showers and others has demonstrated that sustained, lasting change in performance is most likely to occur when teachers participate in a support network with partners. Since it may take more than a year to blend these strategic teaching strategies into daily practice, the participating teachers gather periodically (biweekly or monthly) to swap stories and techniques. In addition, refresher sessions and updates are planned throughout the 18-24 month learning period to augment the introductory sessions. We know enough about pacing new material to steer clear of massive introductory doses. It works better to spread the new material out over time so teachers can adopt and adapt new skills at a comfortable speed.

Chapter 4 - Grazing the Net

Raising a Generation
of Free Range Students

Gathered around a classroom computer monitor, three students are exploring the *Internet* – a global network linking them to vast databases, immense archives, rich art collections and millions of users.

Is this a good thing for schools?

The potential is amazing. An impressive information harvest is just within our grasp. Suddenly we might have all the cultural treasures and the best ideas of human civilization available within a simple mouse click (provided someone digitizes and shares them.)[1]

Schools across North America are rushing to network. Governments and corporations hasten forward with grant support, advice, encouragement, pressure and products. The *Internet* is sold as the bridge to the future. Few dare to raise concerns or to challenge the royal tailors as weavers run cable from classroom to classroom.

The "wired school" is all the rage.

Access to the *Electronic Highway* becomes a priority. Networking schools becomes a goal in itself. For some it becomes an obsession. Bill Gates has compared the rapid development of the Internet to the California Gold Rush of 1849.[2] Some of us remember the miners who returned empty handed.

Billions are diverted from roofing projects, libraries and art programs to bring schools "online."

Is it really worth all the money and the bother?

It is time for educators to ask tough questions about this so-called electronic "miracle."

Will we see dramatic increases in student achievement to justify this investment?

In many cases – those districts that fail to clarify learning goals and fund professional development – the answer will be "No!" There is no credible evidence that networks improve student reading, math or thinking skills unless they are in service of carefully crafted learning programs that show students how to interpret information and make up their own minds.

In the best cases - with the right program planning and robust professional development - schools will use these new tools and resources in ways that will improve student performance on high stakes state tests.

This chapter shows how schools may take advantage of these electronic networks to raise a generation of **free range students** – young people capable of navigating through a complex, often disorganized information landscape while making up their own minds about the important issues of their lives and their times.

The same skills that allow students to make up their own minds will serve them well on Life's tests as well as increasingly challenging state tests.

Students as Infotectives

The first step toward a sound program is to think of students as *infotectives*.

What is an *infotective*? . . . a student thinker capable of asking great questions about data (with analysis) in order to convert the *data* into *information* (data organized so as to reveal patterns and relationships) and eventually into *insight* (information that may suggest action or strategy of some kind).

An *infotective* solves information puzzles with a combination of inference skills and new technologies. The problem solving that often follows the detective work requires synthesis (invention) and evaluation (careful choices from lists of options). An *infotective* is a skilled thinker, researcher and inventor.

Grazing the Net

Infotective is a term designed for education in an Age of Information. In the smokestack school, teachers imparted meanings for students to digest, memorize and regurgitate. In Information Age schools, students make the meaning. They puzzle their way through piles of fragments - sorting, sifting, weighing and arranging them until a picture emerges.[3]

These same skills produce high performance on the increasingly challenging state tests of reading comprehension and problem solving. As state standards require more and more inferential reasoning, state tests are asking students to "create answers" rather than "find answers."

For decades, schools showed students basic problem patterns and asked them to memorize solutions. This approach will no longer suffice. Students are expected to handle the unexpected and the unfamiliar.

Infotectives perform well on demanding comprehension tests, but they also make the kind of workers and family members we need to face the challenges of the next decade and beyond.

Issues of Reliability and Adequacy

We must also give students the tools to overcome the weaknesses of the new information sources.

The extensive information resources to be found in *cyberspace* are both a blessing and a curse. Unless students possess a toolkit of thinking and problem-solving skills to manage the inadequacies of the information landfills, yard sales, gift shoppes and repositories so prevalent on the "free *Internet*[4]," they may emerge from their shopping expeditions and research efforts bloated with techno-garbage, information junk food or info-fat.

Schools must teach students to graze and digest the offerings thoughtfully in order to achieve insight. They must also guide young people away from undue reliance upon the "free Internet." Students will learn that a printed book or a "pay for service" electronic information source[5] will often prove more reliable and efficient than the

Internet.

Towns, universities and schools are learning that they must maintain robust libraries and print collections even in this time of electronic abundance. The new information landscape requires literacy skills well beyond those needed in previous times, and learners soon find that digital sources are insufficient for many questions and topics.

The Question is the Answer

To be successful with this venture, we must emphasize the development of questioning skills, and we must replace topical research with projects requiring original thought.

Questioning may be the most powerful technology we have ever invented and can give to our students. Questions are the tools required for us to "make up our minds" and develop meaning.

Unless we are connecting with the *Internet* for mere *edutainment*[6], student questioning must be intense before, during and after visiting *cyberspace.*[7]

We must teach students to start their explorations with "essential questions"[8] in mind. They then develop a rich web of related questions that organize and direct the search for insight.

Essential questions spawn inquiries that often extend over a month or a lifetime - questions worth asking, that touch upon basic human issues - investigations that might make a difference in the quality of life - studies that might cast light in dark corners, illuminating basic truths.

Once they have listed pertinent questions, we must teach students how to conduct a thorough research study. Questioning persists throughout all stages of such an inquiry as students seek pertinent information . . . data that will cast light upon (or illuminate) the essential question.

Sample Research Question (Secondary)

"Imagine that you and your partners have been hired as consultants by the states of Washington and Oregon to recommend new policies to stem the decline of the salmon runs during the past decade. Use the *Internet*, as well as books, newspapers, interviews and all other appropriate resources, to identify useful practices already tested around the globe, and then determine the applicability of these practices to the particular conditions and needs of the Northwest. How might these strategies be improved? Create a multimedia report for the two governors sharing specific action recommendations as well as the evidence sustaining your proposals."

Unfortunately, schools have traditionally neglected the development of student questioning skills. According to Hyman[9] (1980), for every 38 teacher questions in a typical classroom there is only one student question. Schoolhouse research, sadly, has too often fallen into the "go find out about" category. Topical research ("Go find out about Dolly Madison.") requires little more than information gathering.

We must move past projects that are little more than searches for answers to simple questions. We must stop asking for the educational equivalent of fast food. No more *trivial pursuit*.

Instead of asking elementary students to find out all they can about a particular state or nation, for example, we should be asking them to make a choice.

"Where should your family relocate?"

They compare and contrast several states or cities - sifting, sorting and weighing the information to gain insight, to make a decision or to solve a problem.

Sample Research Question (Elementary)

"Imagine that your parents have been given job offers in each of the three following cities: New Orleans, Seattle and Chicago. Knowing of your access to the *Internet*, they have asked you to help them decide which city will be the best for the family. Before gathering your information, discuss and identify with them the criteria for selecting a home city. Create a persuasive multimedia presentation showing the strengths and weaknesses of each city on the criteria your family considers important."

Conducting the old topical research with electronic information is a bit like pedaling a tricycle on the Interstate. To mix metaphors, classic school research projects (finding out about a particular state) are too much like shooting at sitting ducks. In an age of information abundance (or glut), they may be quasi-suicidal for teachers. Be ready for hundred page research papers that have been downloaded, cut and pasted with relatively little reading, thought or synthesis.

Topical research in this new Information Landscape is the enemy of thought. We are beginning to see a "New Plagiarism" that is simply the old plagiarism abetted by a much more powerful electronic shovel. Stealing other folks' ideas and intellectual property has become much easier. Packaging a paper with a slick appearance has also been simplified.

This decade is the *Age of Glib*. Volume passes for understanding. Surface is preferred to depth. Even adult thinkers (reporters, pundits and commentators) indulge in sound bites, mind bytes, eye candy and mind candy.

If we insist that research focus upon essential questions, we may have an antidote to the New Plagiarism and the *Age of Glib*. We pose questions that require fresh thought. Our students must <u>make</u> answers, not simply gather them.

Great Models for the New School Research

We should take advantage of the good research models now available.

Once they have had a taste of the *Internet*, many teachers express frustration and disillusionment. They seek guidance and mediation. They cannot afford to wade through thousands of "hits" and hundreds of Web pages – most of which are irrelevant, highly commercialized or untrustworthy. They welcome structured research units that will engage students in meaningful and somewhat efficient inquiry.

Fortunately, teachers can now find projects online to deliver solid research. Many of these units are available free over the *Internet* thanks to sponsors such as PacBell and other companies who would like to see the *Internet* a basic element of K-12 education. Others are now available for sale as a new generation of educational publishers emerges.

These projects all require higher level thinking, problem solving and fresh thought. They also provide plenty of scaffolding – supportive structures that help guarantee that student time will be spent productively. There will be little wandering about or "surfing." Teachers can rest assured that students will be challenged and motivated. They will be directed toward reliable and developmentally appropriate Web resources.

Blue Web'N is a PacBell site offering a comprehensive collection of research projects organized into subject areas and grade levels.
URL: http://www.kn.pacbell.com/wired/bluewebn/

WebQuests is yet another PacBell funded site that offers challenging research projects along with online lessons to show teachers how they might build their own projects if they wish. Webquests require that students work as teams to develop solutions to problems and responses to challenges. As more and more teachers find the approach appealing, the collection of projects expands and deepens in quality.
URL: http://edweb.sdsu.edu/webquest/webquest.html

Educational publishers who are providing support for this kind of research at their Web sites include Classroom Connect, Scholastic and CCC (Computer Curriculum Corporation).

Classroom Connect offers a series of research projects called "Connected Questions," all of which require that students make thoughtful choices based upon research conducted with the structure of the Research Cycle.[10]

Grazing the Net

"Would you rather be the Queen of England or the President of the United States? An astronaut or an athlete?"

URL: http://www.classroom.com

Scaffolding may be the best response to the disorganization so typical of the *Internet*. Well organized research units point students to good resources and speed them toward insight.

Creating the Wired Classroom and the Wired School

We can create classrooms that hum with purpose and meaning.

As we approach the new century, we see a new kind of classroom emerging. The "wired" classroom differs dramatically from classrooms of the smokestack era. Given rich information and global communications, students spend their time quite differently. There is no "front" in the wired classroom. The teacher is rarely a "sage on the stage." There is much more facilitating, more supporting, more encouragement and fewer lectures.

One of the best models available to structure the learning in this new kind of classroom is called "Engaged Learning."

According to **Plugging In**[11], we can judge our classrooms "Engaged" when we witness the following indicators:

Engaged Learning Indicators

- Children are engaged in authentic and multi-disciplinary tasks
- Students participate in interactive learning
- Students work collaboratively
- Students learn through exploration
- Students are responsible for their learning
- They are strategic

The teacher in this classroom often acts as a "guide on the side."

The teacher is on the move, checking over shoulders, asking questions and teaching mini-lessons for those who need a particular skill. Support is customized and individualized.

The "guide on the side" sets clear expectations, provides explicit directions, and helps to keep the learning reasonably well structured and productive.

Actions associated with the guide are . . .

circulating	validating	moderating
redirecting	facilitating	diagnosing
disciplining	moving	motivating
encouraging	fascinating	suggesting
guiding	questioning	monitoring
directing	observing	watching
assessing	challenging	seed planting
clarifying	modeling	trouble-shooting

While this kind of activity echoes the classrooms of John Dewey and the Progressives, it differs in the level of structure provided and the richness of the information available. There is more structure, more guidance and a higher level of expectation. There is also far more data to process than ever before.

The ultimate goal is the development of self-directed learners and free-range students, but the path toward that goal is "paved with good intentions and much scaffolding." The presumption independent learning emerges following an investment in skill development over time.

When the *Internet* first came to schools in the mid 1990s, there was much talk of "surfing the Net," but most teachers quickly learned that surfing was little better than strolling through the mall. Schools with significant access have moved to more challenging and rigorous experiences requiring research and reasoning.

Preparing Students for Cyberspace - Internet Competencies

We need to identify and teach literacy skills.

The Internet poses a difficult challenge . . .

How will the voyager know when they have found **Truth**? Answers are a dime a dozen. Insight, on the other hand, is rare. Without some grounding in literacy, we may raise a generation rich in data, facts and information but lacking in wisdom.

"We live in a world where there is more and more information, and less and less meaning."

> Jean Baudrillard
> **Simulacra and Simulation**, 1981

Success in cyberspace requires many of the following skills:

• Framing essential questions

If "the question is the answer," we would expect our students to recognize the important questions of life without waiting for someone else to supply them. They must also be able to state these questions in their own words.

• Identifying subsidiary questions

Great questions spawn countless related questions that suggest an *Internet* path for the researching team. Question webbing is a powerful mapping tool to guide *Internet* voyages. Each voyage will probably suggest new questions as the unknowns become better known. The better the searching, the more the web of questions expands.

• Planning a cyberspace voyage

While it is seductively easy to plunge right into the search for information, advanced planning can save a huge amount of time and speed one toward information that is pertinent and helpful. Mapping out questions is the first stage. Then comes the development of "telling questions" – questions that contain particular elements that produce results as effectively as a "smart bomb."

"How has the FBI violent crime rate changed in the past decade?"

The question contains specific data as well as a source. With these tools in hand, the learner may now take advantage of a guide book or an index such as *Yahoo* to pass directly to an authoritative source such as the Web site for the *Federal Bureau of Investigation* rather than wandering about the entire Web.

• Collecting on the run

Because it is too easy to download hundreds of articles and pages without reading them or thinking about them, the infotective becomes highly skilled at gathering just the *pertinent* information. The infotective collects the most important clues and files them in an organized manner that makes retrieval and synthesis easier at a later time. The infotective usually outgrows a word processor for note taking and opts for a database that will support more powerful searching, sorting and manipulation of data.

```
Source:
Subject Words:
Key Words:
Abstract:
```

The "Source" field is reserved for all the normal bibliographic material required for footnotes and citations. For an Internet site it would include author, title, site name and URL.

The "Subject Words" field is for major categories such as *Crime*, *Weather*, *New Orleans*, *Seattle* and *Chicago*, etc. – concepts that will help to organize the findings later.

The "Key Words" field is for sub categories on a greater level of detail such as *murder*, *robbery*, *assault*, etc.

The "Abstract" field is for entering findings. The student paraphrases and summarizes the most important ideas and information. This is a good place to avoid cut-and-paste.

Wise gathering pays handsome dividends when it comes time to make sense out of the research. Being selective early on means far less time will be required later when it comes time to sort, to sift and to screen the mountains of data.

• Changing course

The journey may lead up blind canyons and sometimes prove frustrating. Effective exploration may require the energy and flexibility of a pinball jumping and bouncing around at incredible speed. Preferably, altering course will be strategic, as the learner watches for trends and tries building theories about where to look, taking advantage of "convergence"[12] to identify the most likely spots to "drill for oil."

• Exploiting serendipity

Even though our culture often conspires to protect us from surprise, much of the power of the *Internet* comes from helping us to escape the boxes within which we live. We have carefully screened out information most of our lives. We are too often the prisoners of our cultures, our educational experiences and our biases. The *Internet* can set us free. It can also drown us in garbage.

• Asking for help

Ranging through dozens of different information sources, the searcher often encounters conflicting and confusing command structures. To prevent gridlock and wasted time, it makes sense to browse the help menu of these sources early in the game.

Many visitors employ Internet search engines such as *HotBot* or *AltaVista* without ever reading the help menu in order to learn the syntax (rules for how to type things) or the advanced features that would make their searching more effective. The extra time spent learning these features will save a hundred fold in what would otherwise become lost time.

• Asking for directions

It makes sense to have several *Internet* guides at the ready and a friend to call when lost. No need to start from scratch. No need to wander in the desert.

• Screening and compacting garbage

TQM (Total Quality Management) has not reached the Net. There is little quality control. Newsgroups overflow with loquacious pedantry and bias masquerading as informed opinion. In smokestack schools students were sometimes urged to reach out toward big page numbers. A good report was a long report. Now it is so easy to download and then cut and paste hundreds of pages of text into a report that it becomes important to cull the essential, meaningful and reliable data. The garbage is set aside, compacted and discarded. The student establishes criteria for reliability and applies them to separate wheat from chaff. Key action verbs: choose, pick, select, separate, sift, and single out.

• Sorting data

In the process of collecting data, students must begin organizing and re-organizing the data in order to find patterns and relationships. This process is the foundation for analysis and synthesis. Key action verbs: align, arrange, array, assort, catalog, categorize, class, classify, cluster, compile, file, grade, group, layout, line up, list, order, organize, outline, pigeonhole, place, position, prioritize, program, rank, stack, tabulate. Associated tasks: bracket, collate, compare, contrast, corre-late, equate, liken, match, and relate.

• Analyzing data

As the data is collected, screened and sorted, the student keeps questioning in order to convert the data into insight. The student approaches understanding - "the big picture" - by undertaking many of the following actions: clarify, interpret, construe, deduce, derive, educe, gather, glean, infer, interpret, surmise, examine, probe, and unravel.

Grazing the Net

• Navigating in the dark

It is no accident that many boat-chartering companies refuse to allow their customers to navigate in the dark. Darkness shifts perception and creates confusing illusions. A vast percentage of the visual cues upon which the casual sailor relies to guide the vessel are eliminated and replaced by a much more challenging system of lights.

At times, the Net provides rich cues to guide one through the shallows and shoals. At other times, it seems like sailing in the dark. Ironically, most essential questions bring us into contact with darkness and the unknown. We often seek illumination for those aspects of our lives that prove most frustrating. The simple answers, the conventional wisdom and the easily accessible recipes are often poor substitutes for the insights that emerge from night sailing. The best navigators learn to sail by the stars.

• Navigating in the mud

When sailors misread the ebbing tide, they may feel the sudden resistance of soft, sucking mud. The *Internet* offers its own information mudflats - vast expanses of soft data and opinion that can bog us down and slow our search for truth. Students must learn to skirt these shoals unless they are prepared to dig deeply and carefully.

• Scanning from the crow's nest

Maintaining perspective is paramount. While conducting research we can be trapped in the day-to-day survival activities occurring at the deck level. We are too close to the action to see the patterns. "Climbing the mast," means stepping outside and above the activities to see them with distance and perspective. The crow's nest allows us to look beyond the ship to ask questions about the challenges and tasks that lie ahead. It means keeping the big picture and the essential questions in mind.

• Creating fresh answers and insight (synthesis)

Students must remember that research is meant to produce new ideas.

This development of fresh answers may be the most difficult task of all. Smokestack schools often required little more than the collection and re-hashing of old ideas and discoveries. Students were rarely challenged to develop original insights.

Now the research "game" has changed dramatically. Intrigued by an authentic question, students find themselves sorting and sifting through the data they have collected, arranging and rearranging the jigsaw pieces and fragments until some picture emerges. They are "on their own." No one shows them the picture on the puzzle box.

There are at least three types of thinking that mix dynamically in a triple-decker combination. All three levels operate concurrently and recursively (like the cat chasing its tail).

1. Envisioning – What is possible?

One type of thought involves conjuring. Identifying possibilities and exploring the unthinkable.

"How could things be changed or made better?"

The students conceive, conjecture, fancy, imagine, project and visualize. Envisioning lifts the product and outcome of the thinking beyond past practice and old thinking. The thinker leaps out of the box of everyday, ho-hum thinking. Of course, grazing the *Internet* lends itself especially well to the encouragement of such flights of fancy. The Net provides excursions, journeys, safaris, sallies, and treks. Envisioning is the source of originality. It provides the energy for change. Cognitive dissonance.

2. Inventing – What needs to be done?

This thinking requires translation of possibilities into actualities.

The imaginative play of the previous type of thinking must be grounded in reality. What might actually work? What is a sensible version of that possibility?

This is the stage at which innovation is born. The student concocts new solutions to problems or coins new ideas and general principles. The research team may hatch a whole new action plan, fabricating and formulating initiatives to clean up local streams. Perhaps the thinking may advance to the development and testing of prototypes before engineering a final product.

3. SCAMPERING and Rearranging – "What if we switch this around?"

The foundation for the two previous functions is the rearranging of the ideas, information and fragments gathered during the research process.

One model for such synthesis is SCAMPER (Eberle, 1997), with each letter standing for a strategy.

S= substitute
C= combine
A= adapt
M= modify, magnify, minify
P= put to other uses
E= eliminate
R= reverse

For this aspect to produce results, the other two aspects must be operating concurrently, as they supply the pressure and cognitive dissonance that inspires creation. The student arranges, blends, combines, integrates, tests, and adjusts the thought fragments until new pictures emerge.

• Suggesting and testing hypotheses

"What if?" thinking helps to propel and inspire mindful, purposeful research through the Net. The student learns to brainstorm multiple explanations and possibilities and then sets out to see which have the most explanatory value.

Grazing the Net

• Opening one's mind

Fundamental to the creation of new knowledge and insight is the process of suspending bias, challenging assumptions and noting premises. The researcher understands that the final product of the search will be made up of three related elements: assumptions, evidence and logic. Ideas have at least three major aspects that can usually be modified and improved:

1. *Ideas are based upon premises* of one kind or another. Many people come to their ideas (judgments or conclusions) without ever explicitly examining the premises that lie underneath those conclusions. Premises are basic beliefs that serve the same purpose for an idea as the foundation of a building or the roots of a tree. Sometimes our thinking comes to us already packaged without our even knowing which premises and assumptions lie below the surface, but an open mind knows that all such premises must be re-examined with some frequency to see if they are serving us well and truly match our basic belief systems.

2. *Ideas are based upon evidence.* Many of our ideas emerge from experience. We collect data, look for patterns and seek laws to help us predict the future. Unfortunately, we all too often collect evidence selectively. An open mind looks at the quality of its evidence with the same dispassionate attitude it applies to its premises and assumptions. The open mind asks, "What evidence do I need to gather? Do I know enough? Has anything changed since I last gathered evidence? Is there new data? Is my data complete?"

3. *Ideas are based upon logic.* Our conclusions and ideas should flow from logical connections between our premises and our evidence. The open mind keeps asking of its ideas, "Is this logical? Does this make sense? Does this follow from the evidence I gathered? Have I identified all the key factors?"

• Seeing what's missing

At times, the enormity of the data cascading into our computers creates the false impression that we have fully explored some topic.

55

Grazing the Net

Experience shows that even when we have mountains of data, we may have missed really important articles or data because we encountered one of the following problems:

1) Flawed search strategies. We pick the wrong search term. Hitting few articles, we conclude that little has been written on that topic. Perhaps if we replace "instructional technology" with "educational technology" we will hit a rich vein of literature. We learn to doubt the efficacy of our search words and use a thesaurus liberally.

2) Biased sources. Even though we would like to believe otherwise, some groups and some aspects of history are systematically avoided or ignored. Imagine a version of U.S. history that never uses the word "broken" in the same paragraph as "treaty." Many sites on the Internet are there because someone has "an ax to grind."

3) Info-Glut. There may be thousands of pages of data that are irrelevant. Conducting an *AltaVista* search with the term "Mayflower," the searcher discovers 22,000 Web pages. Using the REFINE function it turns out that a third of those pages are devoted to restaurants and hotels.

4) Wrong source. Some of the most important information and thinking available to our culture has not been digitized. Other chunks are available only at a price. If you want the best thinking of a medieval monk, you may want to read a hard cover book. If you want the best thinking of an investment guru, you may want to buy a subscription to her online journal.

• Recognizing anomaly

Cyberspace provides a rich offering of anomalies (*American Heritage Dictionary*: deviation from the normal or common order or form or rule; abnormality). These anomalies can be a great source of inspiration and invention during times of rapid change. They are outstanding events. They stand as extra-ordinary. They are, by definition, out of the box. They may be glimpses of our futures. Students can be taught to seek, capture and examine such irregularities, remembering that penicillin was discovered because of a laboratory error that grew a mold by accident. The Internet may offer many powerful accidental discoveries.

Conclusion:
Raising A Generation of Free Range Students

What is a "free range student?"

It is a student who has learned to feed on the wild grains and fragments available on the *Internet* or the shelves of the local library. It is a student *infotective*.

Five years ago when I first wrote this chapter, primed with enthusiasm for the Net, I underplayed the continuing significance of the library, but I have come to see that the *Internet* offers its own share of hormones and chemicals. Freedom lies in offering the widest possible array of information sources, including hard cover books that would never win enough Nielsen ratings to survive on *Prime Time*.

Just as some gourmets prefer free range chickens to their plump cousins, the theme of this chapter is the value of raising children to think, explore and make meaning for themselves. No more second hand knowledge. We work toward more independence and greater choice.

Students learn to make sense out of nonsense and order out of chaos. They ask essential questions and solve complex problems. They join electronically with brothers and sisters around the globe casting a spotlight on earth-threatening issues that deserve attention and action.

When combined with traditional sources, the *Internet* offers remarkable freedom of access to information unless a school or library has chosen to filter, limit and restrict. At the same time, we have learned that Info-Heaven can quickly become Info-Hell if we do not equip our students with the reasoning and exploration skills required to cope with Info-Glut and Info-Tactics. To a large extent, the value of

Grazing the Net

Cyberspace resides in the minds of the voyagers.

Notes

[1] Clifford Stoll points out in Chapter Eleven of *Silicon Snake Oil* (Anchor Books, NY, 1995) that few of these treasures have actually made it into the Internet.

[2] Bill Gates speaking at NECC'97, June 30, 1997

[3] *Power Learning*, McKenzie, Corwin Press, Newbury Park, California, 1993.

[4] We need to distinguish between the sprawling information collection that is available without cost and those (more professional) resources that arrive over the same highway with a price tag attached. There is no "free lunch" on the *Internet*. The best and most reliable information usually requires a "toll" of some kind unless the information is available because of governmental (read "taxpayer supported") funding.

[5] An example would be electronic periodical collections that can be purchased for installation on a school network and made available on every desktop.

[6] *Edutainment* is a term for educational software created with a strong arcade flavor. Many educators question its value as a learning experience.

[7] For a thorough review of the questioning skills students must acquire, consider the October, 1997 issue of *From Now On*. http://fno.org/oct97/question.html

[8] The *Coalition of Essential Schools* introduced this term for questions that are sufficiently intriguing and challenging to sustain a year long (or lifetime) study.

[9] Hyman, Ronald Hyman, R. (1980). Fielding Student Questions. Theory into Practice; 1, pp. 38-44.

[10] The *Research Cycle* first appeared in an article published by *Multimedia Schools*, June, 1995. It was then expanded in a series of articles published in Technology Connection. This series is available online at http://fno.org/oct97/research.html

[11] *Engaged Learning* is fully outlined in *Plugging In: Choosing and Using Educational Technology.*, available from *NCREL* (the North Central Regional Educational Laboratory.) http://www.ncrel.org/sdrs/edtalk/toc.htm Much of the model is based upon the work of Barbara Means.

[12] *Convergence* is a term used by oil prospectors who look for the presence of several prime geological factors all in the same spot to announce the presence of oil.

Chapter 5 - The Information Literate School Community

Networking is not a sufficient goal in itself, as most wired schools quickly learn. This effort is about enhanced performance . . . students who can write, think, reason and communicate more powerfully. If we follow installation with the right kinds of programs and professional development, we should see smarter, more capable students emerge. We should see young people who can solve problems and make up their own minds.

Looking for a clear focus and a clear purpose? Turn your school into an **information literate school community** and count the blessings.

Professional development programs might well make **information literacy** the centerpiece of all adult learning. If all teachers could develop their own information literacy, they might also turn about and nurture the same skills in their students.

Defining Information Literacy

Information literacy has three major components, all of which require that learners "make up their own minds." Mere gathering of information is old-fashioned and obsolete. We expect inventive thinking from students.

1. **Prospecting**: The first component of information literacy relates to the discovery of pertinent information. Prospecting requires navigation skills

as well as the ability to sort, sift and select relevant
and reliable data.

2. **Interpreting**: It is not enough to locate numbers,
   text and visual data. The learner must be able to
   translate data and information into knowledge, insight
   and understanding. The learner must be skilled at
   interpretation.

3. **Creating Good New Ideas**: True information literacy
   includes the development of new insights. We must not be
   satisfied with rehashing the ideas of others. We expect more
   than thinly disguised plagiarism. We expect good ideas.

It may take several years for a school to approach the goal of
universal information literacy. The journey requires a substantial and
sustained commitment to professional development and program
development.

Signs of Progress

How does a school know when it has achieved the status of an
information literate school community? When the following characteristics are abundantly evident, the phrase is well deserved.

• Invention
Much of the school program (25 or more per cent?) is dedicated to
problem-solving, decision-making, exploration and the creation of
new ideas. Both teachers and students are increasingly engaged in the
discovery and building of meaning around challenging questions
drawn from the curriculum.

• Fluency
Teachers move back and forth between an array of instructional
roles and strategies. Sometimes they are the sage on the stage. Other

times they are the guide on the side. They are acquiring an expanding toolkit of strategies.

• Support

The school provides ongoing support for all learners to develop thinking and information skills. These opportunities are rich, frequent and embedded in the daily life of the school.

• Navigation

Learners are developing the agility to find their way through the new information landscape with little lost time.

• Searching

Learners apply Boolean Logic. They search with appropriate syntax. They employ powerful search strategies to carve through mountains of information.

• Selection

Learners know how to separate the reliable from the unreliable source. They recognize propaganda, bias and distortion.

• Questioning

Learners know how and when to employ dozens of different types of questions. Some are best to solve a problem. Others help in making a decision.

• Planning

Learners are acquiring planning and organizational skills. They make wise choices from a toolkit of research strategies and resources. They learn when a particular strategy might produce the best results.

• Interpretation

Learners convert primary sources and raw data into information, and then proceed further (beyond information) to insight. They translate, infer and apply what they have gathered to the issue at hand.

• Deep Thinking

Learners combine deep thinking and reading with a wide-ranging search for relevant information. This quest for information is but the prelude to the more important work . . . solving a problem, creating a new idea, inventing a product or composing a symphony.

• Commitment

All curriculum documents include clear statements regarding the information literacy expectations that are developmentally appropriate for each grade level.

Online Resources

For an excellent overview of information literacy, consult Linda Langford's article, "Information Literacy: A Clarification" in School Libraries Worldwide, Volume 4, Number 1.

http://fno.org/oct98/clarify.html

The American Association of School Librarians (AASL/AECT) provides extensive resources in support of **Information Power: Building Partnerships for Learning** that includes **the Information Literacy Standards for Student Learning**.

http://www.ala.org/aasl/ip_implementation.html

"Information literate school community" appears as a goal in **Learning for the Future: Developing information Services in Australian Schools** (1993), a contemporary standards and guidelines document that could be used to monitor the impact of school library resource centers in a range of educational settings across Australia. Order from: Curriculum Corporation

http://www.curriculum.edu.au/catalog/catlibr.htm)

Part Two

Designing Adult Learning

Chapter 6 - Secrets of Success

The Screen Saver Disease

We have been at it for two decades . . . trying to blend new technologies into the daily life of math, science, social studies and third grade classrooms.

The results? Mixed.

Pioneering teachers love technology and use it with zest. Sages shrug it off and go on with business as usual. In all too many schools, brand new monitors glow in swirling colors while students still grasp pencils, notebooks (paper) and dry lectures. According to several recent studies, technology frequently remains down the hall - a separate, segregated subject.

As noted in earlier chapters, many schools with brand new networks suffer from the **Screen Saver Disease**.

The Good News

We know what works.

We can clarify purpose and then equip a school district with the kind of learning that makes **IL** (Information Literacy) a widely accepted set of tools and resources for all teachers and students.

We have learned encouraging lessons about promoting the growth of teacher enthusiasm and skill.

This book outlines the most effective technology learning practices we have invented during this decade and suggests strategies to blend them throughout the life of your schools. This chapter outlines ten lessons that can help you convert a ho-hum staff development program into a dynamic campaign.

Use these bold stroke design principles to launch your school and your district into the Information Age with broad-based support and impressive skill.

Lesson One
• *Spend 25% or more of the Technology Budget on Staff Learning*
• *Provide 15-60 hours annually per teacher for several years*

The Illinois State Board of Education wisely requires that all technology grant projects now dedicate at least 25 per cent of the project budget to staff learning. Few schools manage 5 per cent according to Market Data Retrieval surveys.

There are no free lunches. The switch from pencil to cursor requires hundreds of hours of exploration and development. If schools do not provide adequate funding for sustained, well-designed adult learning programs, a large percentage of school folks (both staff and students) will not switch tools.

The single biggest explanation for the failure of technologies to penetrate the routines of schools is the failure to fund staff learning on a robust level.

The economics are simple. Better to have fewer computers being used 95 per cent of the time than many more desktops installed but disowned and rebuffed.

Spend less on hardware, more on human infrastructure.

Lesson Two
Clarify Purpose - Problem-Solving & Decision Making

Teachers don't have time for **Trivial Pursuit**.

Give them something worth doing and they are far more likely to grasp the mouse as well as the big picture.

This revolution is more about information than technology. When you emphasize problem-solving with rich information, many techno-holdouts lay aside their reservations.

When you engage teachers in the search for answers to essential questions, they acknowledge the power of information. Focus their adult learning on issues that matter to them, and they see the value of honing student information skills.

> *How do I help my mother adjust to Alzheimer's?*
> *What are the best treatments?*
> *What are the best family strategies?*

Once the district technology plan identifies 3-4 prime learning goals such as *problem-solving*, *communicating* and *decision-making*, the adult learning shows teachers how to bring such goals to life.

Lesson Three
Replace Staff Development and Training with Adult Learning

A few years back a presenter at **ASCD**'s national conference proclaimed "An End to Staff Development."

Staff development is all too often what we **DO TO** teachers. It sets up a parent-child relationship - often inspiring resistance and resentment rather than growth.

Training is what we do to dogs and pigeons.

Choice is the cardinal design concept behind adult learning. Adult learning is an approach that recognizes that people learn most energetically when they have options that match

- their preferences
- their interests
- their styles
- their interests

One size does NOT fit all!

Secrets of Success

The research base behind adult learning (ANDRAGOGY) is a rich source of both potent strategies and proven design standards to increase the success of your technology program.

With this approach, you begin by identifying all life events that might lead to increased learning, significantly broadening the array of sanctioned activities beyond the traditionally limited assortment of classes normally associated with staff development.

Examples . . .

- Visits to information rich work places (e.g.., factories, shipping companies, newspapers, farms, etc.)
- Study groups
- Tutorials
- Invention sessions
- Summer reading
- Free at-home access to computer and online information

The goal is to propose 50-60 compelling activities the district might employ to recruit all teachers for the cause.

Lesson Four
Designate Student Learning as the Cause (not Applications)

The cause? Teaching students how to make up their own minds in this *new information landscape.*

While the new technologies offer far more data than ever before, to convert the mountains of data into insight or knowledge requires remarkable skills . . .

- Questioning
- Navigation
- Information Literacy: inference, analysis, synthesis, interpretation
- Independent thinking

Secrets of Success

Begin with important questions, tasks and projects. Form the adult learning around these tasks. Some examples . . .

What should we do about . . .

acid rain	global warming
urban decay	violent crime
drunken driving	smog
traffic congestion	water pollution
declining fish harvests	endangered species
unemployment	government corruption
health care costs	AIDS
teen pregnancy	racial conflict

How shall I contend with . . .

new developments in my subject area

my parent's illness	my next career challenge
funding my child's college	my needs to learn
my changing relationships	change of various kinds

While exploring these kinds of issues, teachers will learn all of the software necessary to conduct their searches, interpret their findings and present their conclusions.

We call this strategy "just in time learning" instead of "just in case learning."

Too much time has been wasted on teaching computer applications apart from their classroom utilization. Rather than employing a business teacher to "train" social studies teachers in 2000 functions they "might some day" need from a spreadsheet program like **EXCEL**, team them in a tutorial of like-minded teachers with a strong focus on investigation. Make sure one is highly skilled in the software to show them how to "crunch numbers" from the **Census** or whatever data source they might explore in their course work.

Make **IL** (Information Literacy) real to teachers - relate **IL** to their classrooms - and they make **IL** their own.

Lesson Five
Address Emotions and the Challenge of Transfer

The best adult learning programs will place a high priority on developing **confidence**, **comfort** and **calm** along with **competence**.

For many of the techno-holdouts, emotions play a very serious role in blocking acceptance of **IL** (Information Literacy).

- What if I look foolish in front of my colleagues?
- What if I cannot make this program work?
- What if I look foolish in front of my students?
- How long will it take before I feel like an expert?
- How do I fit this into my already crazy schedule?
- How will I find time to cover the curriculum if we're doing so much research?

Even those who are moderately open to using **IL** have concerns about the unpredictability of the **IL** experience.

- What if the Network shuts down in the middle of my class?
- What if the Internet is slow?
- What if my students lose their work?
- What if we can't find any good information on our topics?

Regrettably, too little of the technology staff development delivered during the past two decades paid attention to this dimension.

The work of Bruce Joyce and Beverly Showers has amply demonstrated the risks of ignoring "the challenge of transfer" - that difficult process of translating theories and strategies acquired during workshops into actual classroom practice.

If you want to see **IL** alive and well in your classrooms, you design learning with an emphasis upon comfort and you provide a good percentage of the time available to foster reflection about the steps that will make the new tools, resources and strategies a fixture in the classroom rather than a figment of someone's imagination.

"So what?" we ask. And then, "So what?" again
"What does this all mean? "
"How might I do this - or something similar - with my students? "
"What would it take?"
"What obstacles might I face? How might I overcome those obstacles? What benefits?"

Lesson Six
Create Teams and a Culture of "Just in Time Support"

Joyce and Showers have substantiated the power of peer coaching and extended support systems when teachers are called upon to adopt challenging new strategies.

You should equip one third of your teachers and many of your students with strong **IL** skills so they can provide "Just in Time Support" at any time on any day - when it is needed. No waiting until Thursday afternoon when the next class is scheduled.

Rather than relying upon a few special technology specialists and risking the development of dependency relationships that might actually delay your progress toward IL integration, share, distribute and empower broadly.

- One teacher is great at spreadsheets
- One teacher is great at search engines
- One teacher is great at multimedia presentations
- One teacher is great at global e-mail partnerships
etc.

Create a culture of adult learning and mutual support.

Lesson Seven
Use Surveys and Assessment to Guide Planning

We can only customize and provide a rich menu of learning experiences well matched to our colleagues if we know their 1) preferences, 2) interests 3) styles, and 4) interests as well as their current skill levels . . . their readiness for new stages.

We must regularly and periodically ask teachers about these matters by means of surveys and other assessment instruments. A yearly survey is essential, but a dynamic program gauges staff attitudes and levels of growth far more often - at least at the conclusion of every new learning experience.

It is best to keep such inventories anonymous, grouping the results within each school to provide a clear picture of the needs that reside within that building.

Examples of such surveys can be found at http://www.bham.wednet.edu/tcomp.htm and at http://fno.org/techlife.html and http://fno.org/techsurvey.html

The more complete our picture of our colleagues' needs and preferences, the better the match between the opportunities we will create and the participants whose enthusiastic engagement we hope to enlist. A faithful match is like the warmth and the yeast that cause bread dough to rise (and then rise again even after being punched down).

Lesson Eight
Provide Time for Invention and Lesson Development

Invention is one of the most powerful learning experiences of all. When we invent, we also **OWN** the product and are more likely to "carry it all the way through to market."

In the case of **IL**, teachers are rarely given time to develop unit and lesson plans that would blend both tools and resources into the daily flow of events. Invention allows teachers to translate new possibilities into familiar terms and real contexts. They adjust to local circumstances. They may customize the lessons to create a faithful match with the needs, the preferences and the capabilities of the young learners they serve.

In all too many cases, schools try to circumvent the invention process by purchasing units developed elsewhere, but few of these user friendly packages take root in local soil. Few win enthusiastic commitment from local staff.

"But where do we find the time?" is the classic response.

Once the district defines staff development as **adult learning** and commits a major portion of the technology project budget, **time** for invention and lesson design becomes more readily available.

Invention must take place within reasonably rigorous guidelines in order to provide some degree of quality control. When you combine definitive structures and clear design criteria, invention will stay on track. In some cases, teachers are set free with plenty of time but little scaffolding. Without clarity, there is a risk that the inventions will perpetuate preexisting practice, twisting and contorting new technologies to fit old goals.

Another source of time is the rearrangement of teachers' work life to minimize the number of weekly hours devoted to mindless, unprofessional activities such as lunch duty and hall duty. Efficiencies and redesign in those quarters can free up time for study groups, invention and program development.

Lesson Nine
Hook the Passions of ALL Teachers

A good Country & Western song uses a "hook" to draw us in and keep us connected like a trout on the line. The **hook** is a line that repeats itself until you find yourself singing it or whistling it over and over as you go about your daily routines. The **hook** is usually haunting in its simplicity and its power.

"And I shaved my legs for this?" (Deanna Carter song)

The best hooks have the power to call up basic passions. They strike us "where we live."

Ho-hum staff development provokes yawns.

We will see engagement and commitment from teachers when we show them how they can wield **IL** to explore their passions and dispel their fears. We see growth and risk-taking when folks care about the destination of the journey.

Lesson Ten
Persist!

We are talking about a 3-5 year journey. While we may have some fast learners, the great majority will require sustained support, follow through and funding over several years if we hope to see them welcome the mouse to their classrooms as a tool worthy of as much (if not more) respect than the time-honored (and resilient) piece of chalk and the lectern.

More to Come

Succeeding chapters will expand upon the themes outlined in this chapter, providing examples, success stories and resources to help you sharpen your skills and invent adult learning programs that invite change.

If we do our work well, we will hear few teachers complaining . . . "And I shaved my legs for this?"

Chapter 7 - The Software Trap

Blue Sky High School has more computers than any other school in the state. They have the best ratio of students to computers. Add to both of these facts a history of intensive and well funded staff development for teachers.

What's wrong with this picture? Great equipment, great software and lots of training. On the surface it looks like they have done everything right.

The principal invites us for a visit. She is worried. Something doesn't feel right. Can we come spend a day observing and a second day meeting with staff? She'd like an honest appraisal.

Are we getting a good return on our investment?" she asks a bit anxiously. "Do we need to change our program?"

Driving down the freeway from the airport into the suburbs, we enjoy a startling view of mountains edging sharply into a clear sky. We realize why they call it "Blue Sky High School."

A student guide greets us and begins the tour. Each department has a computer lab. The business department has three.

We walk into the science computer lab. No students. Glowing screens. Screensaver disease.

"Probably an off day," our guide comments smoothly and reassuringly, well schooled at 17 in the art of public relations.

"Is there a schedule for the lab?"

Looking at the schedule posted on the wall, we see that the lab is scheduled 25% of the available class periods. It is empty 75% of the time and only 3 of the 12 science teachers are using it that week.

Evidently an off week.

The Software Trap

We go down the hall and find every lab empty except for computers and glowing screens. Equipment galore. We encounter little use until we reach the business labs that are humming and fully scheduled. Each student is busy learning how to use four different kinds of spreadsheets as well as an arsenal of other applications.

The next day we meet with teachers during prep periods. They are proud of their training, but they confess some distaste for the software in their labs and some confusion about purpose. Most of them complain that computers seem peripheral. Some use the word "frivolous."

"Since your students have learned to use 4 spreadsheets and you have learned 3 spreadsheets, can you give us some examples of how you have asked your students to use spreadsheets in your science or math or social studies classes?"

The question is met with silence . . . sideways glances . . . awkwardness.

Three of the 120 teachers can report the use of spreadsheets in class. The school has prepared students and staff to employ spreadsheets but failed to identify their value for schooling and learning.

We complete our diagnosis . . .

"This school suffers from the 'software trap.'"

The Software Trap

Blue Sky High School (a fictitious name) had fallen into the trap of confusing software programs with purpose. The high school operated on the premise that teachers would integrate technologies into the regular classroom if they just had enough time to learn basic software programs such as ClarisWorks or Microsoft Excel.

In making this assumption, the school effectively placed the cart before the horse and ignored the most important learning issue of all, which is how to use these technologies to enhance student thinking and performance.

Sadly, when asked to produce their technology professional development program, many schools display a list of classes in as-

The Software Trap

sorted software programs . . .

1. Introduction to Word
2. Intermediate Word
3. Advanced Word
4. Introduction to the Internet
5. Advanced Internet
6. Introduction to PowerPoint
7. Advanced PowerPoint
8. Introduction to Web Publishing
9. Advanced Web Publishing

After 20 years of working with this strategy, most reports indicate that the majority of teachers have still not integrated new technologies into their classrooms.

The approach, while popular, is flawed because it ignores the most important needs of teachers. It fails to address the teaching and learning issues that are central to the challenge of blending these tools into daily classroom activities.

The 10 Myths Behind the Software Trap

The focus on software applications is based a curious mythology that ignores most of what we know about maximizing adult learning while encouraging shifts in behavior.

Myth 1

Knowledge of software translates into the delivery of technology rich lessons. Additional hours of software training translate into additional hours classroom usage.

Reality

Software may change classroom lessons if teachers identify "entry points" that will improve student performance. A spreadsheet may enhance the study of acid rain if the teacher can see where the tool fits into the gathering and analyzing of field data. On the other hand, if the teacher never asks students to interpret data, the tool will rust in a corner.

Myth 2

Teachers respond best to instructors who are super skilled in the application.

Reality

Many teachers, especially the reluctants and late adopters, are looking for comfort and reassurance. In many cases, a razzle-dazzle software teacher may intimidate learners. Sometimes "less is more." Warm support and encouragement are often more important than skill. Awareness of curriculum and classroom "entry points" may be more important than mastery of software features. A track record of successful classroom experience is critically important.

Myth 3

Classes are the most productive adult learning system.

Reality

Given a choice, many teachers vote for small group tutorials, study groups, individual study and informal learning opportunities over formal classes. Classes rarely address the concerns and interests of teachers and often leave them asking, "How do I use this with students?"

Myth 4

Teachers cannot teach themselves software.

Reality

Classes too often foster dependency. While early adopters and pioneers teach themselves most of what they know about technologies, late adopters are prone to wait for more classes and more training. We show teachers how to learn programs independently. And we should give them support and encouragement to do so.

Myth 5

Skills are primary and feelings are secondary.

Reality

We know that human learning engages both the cognitive and the affective domains, but much technology training ignores feelings, anxieties and human needs while outlining skill goals that may be overwhelming. Participant comfort, confidence and competency should always stand high in the list of course design criteria.

Myth 6

This is about technology, not teaching and learning.

Reality

The bottom line for most teachers is student performance. This focus intensifies as states elevate curriculum standards and introduce increasingly demanding tests. Few teachers see technology as a goal and need to see how it might contribute to their bottom line. They want to see how technology might make their students better writers, readers and thinker. They don't care much whether they are good word processors.

Myth 7

One size fits all: learning styles, pacing and developmental differences do not matter.

Reality

Participants in skill-based software classes often spread out across a broad continuum of readiness and preparedness that usually means that the instructor is almost doomed to move too fast or too slow for someone. Differences in learning styles also mean that the choices are essential to provide a good match between learner and experience – choices that are rarely possible during software classes.

Myth 8

Learning is most productive when experienced out of context.

Reality

The teacher's most important context is the classroom. More precisely, a social studies teacher's context is a social studies classroom. Even though the teacher needs to know how to use the tools within the classroom context, software classes are almost always generic, K-12 experiences that ignore the classroom issues of the participants. The instructor rarely knows anything about the challenges of teaching middle school social studies and can provide no cogent examples of how a spreadsheet might enhance student learning within such a context.

Myth 9

Teachers cannot consider classroom issues unless they are first firmly grounded in all of the software programs.

Reality

Groups of early adopters and late adopters may gather as invention teams to create technology rich unit plans and lesson plans. Late adopters prove valuable participants even though they may not possess advanced software capabilities because they can contribute good curriculum suggestions. During the invention process, late adopters will usually pick up many technology skills and will gain confidence and enthusiasm for the potential of these tools to change their classrooms. Holding them back at introductory levels is patronizing, demoralizing and wasteful.

Myth 10

There are no other options.

Reality

This book outlines more than a dozen adult learning strategies, most of which emphasize curriculum, learning and student performance. It is clear that curriculum and strategic teaching should take precedence over equipment and software. We need to untie the cart and place it where it belongs . . . behind the four horses of curriculum, learning, teaching and exploration.

We need to know what is working, what is not working and what needs changing. Without a robust and authentic assessment model, we are steering in the dark. We have little basis to invent, to modify or to shift direction. We surge ahead with Titanic confidence, entirely unaware of ice flows awaiting us in the darkness ahead.

"Ignorance is bliss until icebergs appear suddenly under your bow."

We also need to show our patrons – the taxpayers and our families – that a robust investment in professional development pays great dividends when it comes to technology. We need to show them that our staff is growing in confidence and skill, that teachers are using the new technologies in powerful ways that promote student achievement and problem-solving abilities.

Few school districts collect or analyze assessment data for either students or staff. But the time has come. According to **the New York Times**, Linda Roberts, Director of the Office of Educational Technology at the Department of Education, stressed the importance of assessment at an April, 1998 conference on schools and technology in Manhattan.

"It's important to collect baseline data and to track performance deliberately."

http://www.nytimes.com/library/tech/98/04/cyber/articles/27education.html

Gauging Return on Investment

"School districts will be called to task for 'What are you doing with your money and what difference does it make?'"

With a reasonable investment of time and money, we can learn a good deal about our colleagues and their responses to our professional development offerings. The better job we do of assessing, the better the match between program and participant. We use what we learn to enrich, enhance and upgrade our offerings.

Gathering the Data

The first step in the process is the selection and/or development instruments and surveys. Fortunately, the best may be home made and home grown, easily adapted to meet changing program needs and purposes.

Doug Johnson, the Director of Libraries and Technology for the Mankato (MN) Schools, was an early pioneer in this effort. He developed a user-friendly scale that has been adopted and modified by many districts to match their program goals.

(To see an adapted version, visit the Bellingham Public Schools Web site at http://www.bham.wednet.edu/tcomp.htm)

Starting with this model, you can add and delete items as you identify those aspects of staff performance that matter most. If, like many districts, you place a premium on **information literacy**, for example, you might develop an item like the following . . .

X. Information Searching

___ Level 1- I am unlikely to seek information when it is in electronic formats.

___ Level 2 - I can conduct simple searches with the electronic encyclopedia and library software for major topics.

___ Level 3 - I have learned how to use a variety of search strategies on several information programs, including the use of "logical operators" such as "AND" and "OR" to help target the search and find just the right information in the most efficient manner. I can perform such searches to locate books and videos with the library software on my desktop.

___ Level 4 - I have incorporated logical search strategies into my work with students, showing them the power of such searches with the encyclopedia or the library software, for example, to locate information that relates to their questions.

In addition to surveys that assess staff skill levels, there are measures of learning styles, preferences and intersts. One example is the **Technology in My Life Survey** (http://fno.org/techlife.html).

For each item, the respondent tells whether they 1) strongly agree 2) agree 3) are not sure 4) disagree or 5) strongly disagree. These three items help to identify the preferred learning mode of the teachers:

9. I prefer to learn new things as an individual.

10. The best way to learn new technologies is to participate in formal training classes that show us just how to use programs and how to apply them to our classes.

13. I do best with new programs and approaches when I can learn them with a partner.

In a more rigorous (and perhaps threatening?) manner, some organizations such as ISTE (The International Society for Technology in Education) are developing performance measures that test teacher competency. http://www.iste.org/Projects/Tech_Standards

These standards have been adopted by the National Council for Accreditation of Teacher Education (NCATE), the official body for accrediting teacher preparation programs.

We will see more instruments and measures emerge in the next two years as technology assessment has becomes a priority for many organizations, including the Department of Education.

"Developing Educational Standards" is a useful annotated list of

Gauging Return on Investment

Internet sites with K-12 educational standards and curriculum frame-works documents, maintained by Charles Hill and the Putnam Valley Schools in New York. http://putwest.boces.org/StSu/Technology.html

Analyzing the Data

When the surveys are administered yearly, a portrait of the staff and its professional development needs emerges – a portrait that guides program planning while showing change over time.

The staff of most schools will report quite a "quilt" of needs, with teachers spread out in clusters along the path toward confident and fully integrated use. This "spread" is usually ignored by the "one size fits all" approach so often taken. Clear data demand more responsive and diverse offerings of learning experiences so that each teacher might find "the right stuff."

Competency	% at Level 1	% at Level 2	% at Level 3	% at Level 4
Operations	0	10	45	45
File Management	5	25	45	25
Word Processing	0	15	55	30
Spreadsheets	15	35	30	20
Databases	25	35	25	15
Graphics	10	45	35	10
Internet Use	30	40	15	15
Telecommunications	30	45	20	5
Ethics	0	15	45	40
Searching	15	45	25	15
Presenting	20	50	20	10
Integrating	15	35	30	20

The data above highlight program elements that require attention and indicate that the staff members are quite different from one another.

Gauging Return on Investment

Does anyone care?

It only makes sense to gather data if there is a planning group whose responsibility it is to develop the long term "grid" of learning opportunities to match the "quilt" of needs mentioned earlier.

Each school should have a team that plans 18-24 months out into the future, identifying resources, experiences and opportunities to speed their colleagues on their way. Without such a team, the professional development offerings may suffer from the "last minute" syndrome.

They review the data and explore key questions such as these:

1. Which program elements are progressing most encouragingly?
2. Which elements require the most attention?
3. How many different "clusters" of learners are there for each learning priority and how might each cluster's needs be met?
4. What are the preferred learning styles within each cluster and how might those styles be accommodated?
5. What resources already exist to support these professional development needs?
6. What new resources must be found and added to the collection available to support staff learning?

Sharing the Results

While program design is the most important use of assessment, we must also share the success story inside and outside of school.

Take advantage of the data to help colleagues celebrate their accomplishments.

Show your patrons – the taxpayers and your families - that teachers are using the new technologies in powerful ways to promote student achievement and problem-solving abilities.

The chart reproduced below shows real data from an elementary school that used the Mankato Scale for three years.

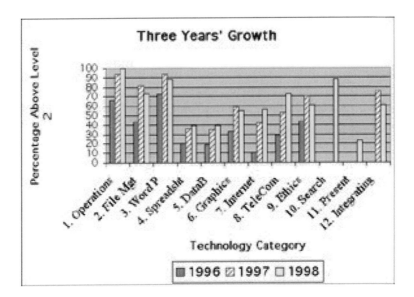

Note: Items 10 and 11 were added in the third year. In some cases, the third year results declined when teachers redefined their notions of high performance after learning more about what was possible.

Conclusion

As much as assessment has been neglected by technology pioneers during the past decade, it will become a major priority during the next three years as districts now recognize the need to demonstrate results as they invest heavily in networks and equipment. Those districts that develop a model dovetailed with the professional development program will find that the investment can pay rich dividends in terms of invention and staff learning.

Chapter 9 - Creating Learning Cultures

The best way to win widespread use of new technologies is to provide **just in time support** . . . assistance and encouragement when needed. Not tomorrow. Not next week. Now!

If schools expect to see a solid return on technology investments, they must foster (and fund) cultures intent on continuous learning and change. But good intentions are not enough. High expectations must be accompanied by substantial resources, most of them human, many of them costly. Help lines, coaches, mentors, partners, study groups and **TIME**!

Integrating new technologies into the daily life of the classroom requires such skill and courage that it simply will not happen across the board in all classrooms unless safety nets are constantly and conveniently available. The integration challenge is more about attitude and spirit than skill.

This chapter suggests a dozen ways to foster growth while whetting appetites for change.

Less Training and More Learning

We need less training and more learning. Many schools are finding success when professional growth and development occur daily . . . just in time! Real learning takes place (or stops) when actually trying the new skills. Just as the teacher is apt to experience surprise, frustration and disillusionment, support must be close at hand.

The old approach of after school technology training sessions does not work. Such sessions demonstrated the features of software applications but rarely showed how to use them in classrooms.

Creating Learning Cultures

The best thinkers about change in schools (Lieberman, Joyce, Loucks-Horsley, Fullan and Deal) emphasize the importance of informal support structures and the cultivation of a learning culture.

In the 1990 ASCD Yearbook, **Changing School Culture through Staff Development**, Fullan states, "The ultimate goal is changing the culture of learning for both adults and students so that engagement and betterment is a way of life in schools."

No more excuses!

If we spend millions on a network, we expect to see it used vigorously and meaningfully. No matter what classroom we visit, we should observe students and teachers leaning intently toward the rich information on the computer screens . . . pointing, questioning, divining meaning, building answers, making choices, solving problems.

A Culture Promoting Adult Learning

Fullan sums up the challenge . . .

"The agenda then is to work continuously on the spirit and practice of lifelong learning for all teachers."

School cultures have not traditionally honored the principles of adult learning. These principles are fully outlined at **Adult Learning Theory: A Resource Guide** (Teresa Kirkpatrick).

http://odin.indstate.edu/level1.dir/adultlrn.html

The clearest way to contrast **adult learning** (often called "**andragogy**") with **pedagogy** (instructor directed learning) is to note that adult learning usually involves the learner in activities that match that person's interests, needs, style and developmental readiness.

Fundamental beliefs:

1) **The learner may make choices** from a rich and varied menu of learning experiences and possibilities.

2) **Learners must take responsibility for planning. acting and growing**.

If we shift school cultures to support adult learning, professional development is experienced as **a personal journey of growth and discovery** that engages the learner on a daily and perhaps hourly basis. In the best cases, andragogy includes an emphasis upon self-direction, transformation and experience. One learns by doing and exploring . . . by trying, by failing, by changing and adapting strategies and by overcoming obstacles after many trials.

Strategy One: Outlining the Journey

Every teacher and administrator creates a technology **TRIP-TIK** - a written PGP (professional growth plan) outlining the best route to **powerful practice.**

The process begins with assessment. Where am I now? Perhaps each person completes a survey like the **Mankato Scale.**

http://www.bham.wednet.edu/tcomp.htm

This activity helps them identify areas deserving the most attention. The teacher then selects from a rich and varied menu of opportunities to help them meet their goals.

Each person commits to try new skills and tools with students in classrooms. The building administrator commits resources and support. They meet regularly to discuss progress.

"How's it going? Anything I can do to help? Any barriers I can remove?"

Strategy Two: Study Groups

Every teacher joins a study group. Three or more in a group. Common interests. Common goals. Self-selected partners with trust and compatibility.

Weekly get-togethers. Like a book group. Exploring new and better ways of teaching. The group poses questions and tries to build answers. They share tricks and tips and resources and stories.

"Anybody find any good biology Web sites since we last talked?"

Learning continues between sessions. Research. Reflection. Questioning. Experimentation. Trial and error. Struggle. Accomplishment. Ongoing.

Creating Learning Cultures

Strategy Three: Technology Coaches

Every teacher becomes a technology coach. Good at somet aspect of technology. Prepared to help others accomplish what they desire. The staff agrees upon 30-100 "talents" and carves them up so that everybody can make a contribution.

The best strategy is to share responsibility broadly. One person specializes in crunching numbers with spreadsheets to understand relationships. Another teacher becomes skillful with search engines and information problem-solving. Yet another concentrates on publishing student work on the Web.

"The more the merrier!"

In the past we have put too much stock in technology specialists and staff developers whose main job was to "train" others in how to use various software programs. They were the experts. The rest of us were "users." This strategy often backfired and caused resistance as well as resentment.

Strategy Four: Technology Mentors

Mentor programs are more structured than coaching . . . a short term pairing of a teacher highly skilled in some practice with one less skilled.

As a result of the self-assessment conducted in Strategy One, a teacher selects a mentor for those areas deserving attention, preferably a trusted colleague, one who will make the mentored teacher feel comfortable.

For these programs to work, there must be a considerable pool of mentors from which teachers may make a choice. A broad pool increases the likelihood of good matches, without which learning is likely to crawl.

Prima Donnas and stars rarely make good mentors. They can be intimidating and off-putting. Knowledge and skill are less important than empathy and nurturing qualities.

Creating Learning Cultures

Strategy Five: Workplace Visits

"Seeing is believing!"

Trite but true. Information is what fuels the economy and the society. For teachers to grasp the dramatic impact of information technologies in the workplace and society, they must spend time visiting as participant observers.

Telling doesn't work. They must see it for themselves.

Organize visits to information rich work places (factories, shipping companies, newspapers, farms, etc.). Teachers spend the first half of the day exploring, watching, questioning, interviewing and recording the role of information technologies and skills in the organization they are visiting. The second half of the day is devoted to reflection.

"So what? What did we learn? What are the implications for schools and our students? What do we need to do to prepare students for this kind of work?"

Strategy Six: Tutorials

Short bursts of learning onsite are perfect for busy teachers. Fifteen minutes here. Ten minutes there. Brief lessons on discrete skills and maneuvers offered by a trusted colleague in a comfortable, small group setting.

Two or three days a week there are early morning lessons on simple tasks like organizing bookmarks files or printing form letters or labels. In the spirit of "just in time learning," the agenda for these quick tutorials would be based upon frequent surveys of staff.

"Given the following list of tasks that can be performed with our technologies, which three are highest on your wish list for a brief tutorial session this month?"

Tutorials offer comfort, convenience, usefulness and immediate results.

Creating Learning Cultures

Strategy Seven: Student Aides

Many teachers worry about technology breakdowns, disappointments, embarrassments and jams of various kinds. They hear horror stories and don't want to experience them.

"What if the printers don't work?"
"What if the system goes down?"
"What if the Internet connection is slow?"
"What if they start looking at dirty pictures?"

No one wants to be left hanging with 30 adolescents wondering why nothing is working the way it's "spozed to be."

No one wants to end up as what one author called "Roadkill on the Information Highway."

We know that many students of our students are quite capable when it comes to making technologies perform the way they are intended. They may not be especially skilled at promoting the curriculum (the teacher's role), but they can provide troubleshooting and support to get us past the many day-to-day breakdowns, bumps and pot-holes. Talk about "just in time learning!"

Develop a (gender balanced) cadre of technology savvy student aides and make sure the teachers know who they are, but make sure you select students who have empathy, tact and warmth as well as skill. This is no time for the "Revenge of the Nerds!"

Strategy Eight: Help Lines

Teachers should be able to call for HELP when they need it. More "just in time learning."

When you get stuck, you pick up the phone, dial a number and ask, "What do I do now?"

How many teachers have telephones in their classrooms, let alone Internet-connected computers?

Many districts wisely install phone systems at the same time they install data networking. They then make sure a techno-savvy educator is "on call" at all times to make sure teachers can keep moving forward with their lessons.

"But where do we find the money?"

So many districts spend a fortune on the infrastructure and hardware while nickel-and-diming the human side of the technology initiative. Failure to staff the human support and infrastructure side will lead to the "Screensaver Disease" mentioncd previously.

Strategy Nine: Invention Sessions

Many teachers hunger for the time to translate new ideas and strategies into practical classroom lessons and unit plans. Invention is the time when teachers take ownership. They make the innovation real. Theory into practice.

If we want to see robust integration, we must provide each teacher with a week or more of invention time each year - whole days away from the pressures of classroom teaching to create worthwhile, technology enhanced learning experiences for students.

Strategy Ten: At-Home Alone (Access)

Many teachers want to stumble privately. They don't want to appear foolish or incompetent in front of their peers. They want to retire into their own classroom or take a computer home to see what they can do. There is so little time in a teacher's life to explore new possibilities. Those who are committed and industrious stay late into the afternoon or evening preparing for the next day or the next week. Some districts have made a swap of time for equipment. The teacher agrees to 60 hours of professional development activities outside the normal schedule as a way of acquiring a new, Internet capable laptop.

Strategy Eleven: Summer/Weekend Reading

"If you buy, they will read . . . "

Creating Learning Cultures

Simple but true. Offer teachers a choice of three or four books from a list of 10-20, and they are likely to devour those books on their own time. If you want to inspire teachers to integrate new technologies into their classrooms, buy them books that tell the stories and the secrets of successful integrators. If you want them to learn the ins and outs of Web publishing, buy them books like "Killer Web Sites."

Strategy Twelve: Distance Learning

Some teachers are more apt to let down their hair, talk honestly and share their anxieties with strangers. They may never confess true feelings to someone down the hall, but they might share deep feelings with someone on the other side of the country.

The incredible lightness of strangers! People will tell a "perfect stranger" their deepest secrets at a bar. Listservs, bulletin boards and chat rooms seem to provide some of the same freedom.

Conclusion

Transformation of schools to make robust and fully integrated use of new technologies represents a major shift in practice. We will not get there by offering training sessions. We must reconceptualize professional development so that we create learning cultures that make change and growth a daily reality.

Online Resources

Practices that Support Teacher Development: Transforming Conceptions of Professional Learning, Lieberman, Ann.
http://www.teachnet.org/ntpi/library/prac/PRAC01.HTM

Research You Can Use. Close-Up #12. Staff Development. Chick, J.S.
http://www.nwrel.org/scpd/sirs/6/cu12.html

Chapter 10 - Invention as Learning

"I need time to figure this out . . . time to invent something that will actually work in my classroom on Monday morning."

A Time for Every Purpose

Districts should spend approximately half of their professional development budgets on time for teacher invention. When teachers are encouraged to build technology-enhanced lessons and units, new technologies find a welcome mat awaiting their arrival and installation. They pass from "intruder" status to "partner" status.

"When are you going to supply enough equipment so we can really make this program hum?"

The creation of a vigorous teacher invention program is a rewarding path to technology acceptance and program integration. This professional development strategy may even engage some teachers who have seemed reluctant in the past.

Teachers deserve a chance to convert theory into practice. As they invent, they can customize lessons to match their own students' needs. They also end up feeling pride of ownership. The new unit is "their baby." They emerge from the invention workshop with a vested interest in seeing the results of their efforts. They want to be present in the delivery room.

Invention as Learning

What is an Invention Workshop?

1. Teams

Teachers gather together for a day or more. They meet with great resources and a clear purpose. Often they work in teams, but they may also split off to create their own individual lesson and unit plans.

Some of the best invention workshops take place during summer months when staff can focus on the design process without worrying about lesson plans for substitutes or the press of classroom obligations.

Working in teams offers the advantage of mixed skill levels and a good deal of informal learning.

2. Lesson Development

In the Grand Prairie ISD, for example, six or seven teachers combined with library media specialists from each grade level to build online Web-based research modules. These projects were designed to match existing curriculum topics while introducing students and other staff members to the power of electronic information.

Within each team there were experts and novices. In addition, the district provided technology coaches and outside consulting support within the workshop setting so that each team might extend its resources when necessary. Throughout the first day, this mixture of skills led to intense informal learning as each team worked on its unit.

The goal was creation of lesson plans to structure a student research investigation that might extend over 7-8 class periods and would require higher level thought. In order to develop such lessons, the inventors engaged in a number of tasks that were new to many of the team members.

To see examples of their work, visit http://www.gpisd.org/gpisd/modules/modulepage.html Baltimore County (MD) and Bateman's Bay in New South Wales have also had success. See http://fno.org/module/module4.html

3. Just in Time Learning

One task was **prospecting** - the search for appropriate electronic information resources to support the student research projects. Because some of the participants in GPISD had never used search engines or search strategies, their partners quickly introduced them to such skills in the course of prospecting for the unit.

One group set off in search of Web sites devoted to Texas heroes. Another went looking for information on Native American tribes from the Texas plains.

Instead of learning these important information skills in isolation, team members acquired them naturally in service to the invention process. The day was rich with "just in time learning."

An invention workshop usually extends over more than one day, depending upon the complexity and scope of the project. Activities should be structured so that this time is spent fruitfully, and the invention process is guided by standards to ensure quality.

Why does Invention work?

1. Understanding

The invention process requires teachers to analyze learning experiences in great depth, breaking them down into components and noting how they relate to each other before reassembling them into a new version appropriate for their own classrooms.

Creating lesson plans requires a level of understanding vastly different from that required during most staff development lessons that show teachers effective practices. When faced with the challenge of making something work with real children in a real classroom, the teacher asks nuts and bolts questions.

Theory is grand, but classroom realities require a very practical look to determine which strategies will work with Sally or Dan and Natasha. The best way to fashion effective lesson plans is to try the activities, role playing student tasks and adjusting the elements of the plans until all flows smoothly and well.

2. Match

Unlike packaged programs and imported programs, inventions are developed with particular classrooms in mind. They are customized to match the needs, interests and abilities of those who will enjoy them.

3. Ownership

Teachers who construct their own units end up caring about their success. These plans, strategies and tools become part of their teaching repertoires. Once they take the time to figure out the puzzle, they feel proud of their accomplishment, and along with pride comes the desire to share. These lessons are unlikely to sit on any shelves because there has been too great an investment of energy and self for them to languish unused.

4. Familiarity

Familiarity breeds . . . comfort and calm. Having lived with the nuts and bolts of the unit during its birth process, the inventors know every detail like the backs of their own hands. Unlike so many packaged technology programs brought into schools, homemade programs can still fears and quiet anxieties.

What elements are required to achieve success?

The invention process is no slam-dunk. There are risks to setting the process in motion. Chief among the dangers is the tendency of some districts to provide little in the way of expectations that might serve to inspire quality.

1. Structure

The clearer the structure provided for the inventors, the greater the likelihood that products will be worth the investment of district funds and professional development time. Structures guide toward quality without restricting or limiting creativity and originality.

2. Models & Exemplars

It helps enormously if teachers can see examples of what other teachers have created and step through an online learning experience, which highlights the key features, and elements of what it is they are expected to build together.

One example - The Module Maker - can be found at http://fno.org/module.html

This set of Web pages was used to introduce teachers in the Grand Prairie ISD to the concept of research modules. It clarified expectations and provided the scaffolding they needed to know how to proceed.

Another example can be found at WebQuests. http://edweb.sdsu.edu/webquest/webquest.html

Enjoy the many offerings of successful research projects as well as online resources that show teachers how to build units.

3. Standards

Quality also emerges when the criteria for success are explicitly stated and then emphasized at the beginning of the invention process. Too many project leaders will skip over this step to their later regret, as mediocre products can easily result.

There is always some danger that tradition may undermine good results. A long history of topical research projects, for example, can lead to the development of units that are little more than 1950s assignments dressed up in electronic threads.

The WebQuest team offers **A Rubric for Evaluating WebQuests** at http://edweb.sdsu.edu/webquest/webquestrubric.html that makes the characteristics of a strong unit plan quite evident.

4. Checkpoints

As a team moves through the planning and development stages, a lead teacher or supervisor with strong program skills should hold periodic conferences with the team at key points to help them stay on track and maintain quality. Especially for those who may be working for 3-5 days, it is foolish to allow several days to pass without providing feedback and support. Checkpoints help ensure that forward movement is productive and appropriate.

5. Resources

In addition to providing adequate time, the next most important resource for teachers is knowledge. In order to protect a team from re-inventing a (stone) wheel, consultants can inform the group of best practices and research findings from around the world. These may be internal or external consultants but providing broadened perspective is their prime purpose.

6. Quality Control

A high level of quality must be reached before a unit is released for publication and classroom use. A leader or a committee with good skills, knowledge, tact and authority should work with each team to make sure they understand what is required before the work is approved for implementation. This is not an easy task because it may cause hard feelings to suggest that a group has more work to do.

Invention is the parent of integration!

Chapter 11 - Online Learning

When we see little return on investment, we look for change.

When it comes to technology, we need big changes in how we offer professional development, and we need them fast.

Driving Forces

To appreciate the import of the new strategies, note the context and the driving forces that brought us to a place where online learning has become especially attractive.

1. A Poor Track Record

Even though we have been trying to bring technology into classrooms for two decades, much of the staff development has been ineffective. The track record is unimpressive. Most reports show a failure to penetrate daily practice in an integrated manner. Educational technologies remain tangential to most classrooms. Many teachers and schools earnestly seek new models that might lead to more impressive results.

2. Too Much Training

As noted in the chapter on the software trap, the professional development offerings have been slim, at best, and are usually dominated by a training model rather than a learning model. We run folks through a linear sequence designed to introduce them to all the neat functions they can perform with the tool at hand. We may even offer practice. What we rarely do is show them how the tool might improve student learning in social studies, science or math.

The training model also suffers from the way it treats the learners. The trainer takes most of the responsibility. The participant makes few choices and exercises little autonomy. The workshop leader determines the pacing. There is little customization. "One size fits all."

3. Too Much Technology

For too long we have emphasized how to use the technology. We have shown teachers the features of software applications but left out the most important issue of all . . . how to use the technology in support of student learning, thinking and problem solving.

For too long we have trained teachers to use technology for technology's sake, as if good spreadsheet skills were an important component of good classroom instruction. It turns out that spreadsheets can help us crunch complex number sets, but "crunching" only helps teachers in their classrooms if number "crunching" is part of the curriculum.

4. Resource Issues

Adults grow increasingly impatient with sitting in classes. They seek other pathways and methods to develop skills and competencies . . . delivery systems to suit their busy life styles. They look for learning that can take place on the run, at any time and in just about any place. No more judging progress by counting the hours of seat time. Competency based learning is rapidly replacing the old model.

In competency based learning, the learner persists until the concept or skill is mastered before moving on. Pretests protect against relearning material already mastered. Post-tests certify when it is time to move forward.

Online Learning

5. Software

Web browsing programs such as **Netscape** or **Internet Explorer** provide support for a new kind of learning. The central metaphor for this approach is "learning as journey." Web pages provide a series of steps for the journey while suggesting side trips and excursions. In addition to enjoying a rich menu of choices, learners control the pacing and customize the experience to match skill levels and style preferences.

Examples

Online learning is emergent. While quite a few software companies are rushing products forward to support the development of online learning for corporations and higher education, K-12 examples are just now appearing.

• WebQuests

The **WebQuest** site funded by PacBell provides online resources that show teachers how to construct their own web-rich research units. No need to attend class. Visit http://edweb.sdsu.edu/webquest/webquest.html for all the tools you need to build your own unit.

• Asymetrix

Formed by early Microsoft founder, Paul Allen, **Asymetrix** is a high tech think tank that has created a product called the **Librarian**. http://www.asymetrix.com/products/librarian/ **Librarian** greets a learner when logging onto a web site and helps them complete their own personal learning journey. The software "interface" keeps track of progress, provides a rich menu of choices and offers tests at key check points when the learner is ready to demonstrate competence or understanding.

While much of the **Asymetrix** effort is focussed upon corporate and higher education learners, the company has its eyes on the K-12 learner, developing prototypes to support AP courses.

Online Learning

• From Now On

During the past few years I have been creating online professional development modules for school districts and several of these can be found at http://fno.org.

1) **Module-Maker** - A self-instructional, online course showing how to create student online research modules.
http://fno.org/module/module.html

2) **Bilingual Online** - Creating Online Resources to Support Bilingual and ESL Programs
http://fno.org/bilingual.html

3) **500 Miles** - Setting Up Year Long Research Projects for Students
http://fno.org/500miles/persistence.html

• Australia

In part because of the huge distances separating cities and developed regions in Australia, distance learning has flourished.

The Center for Teacher Librarianship at Charles Sturt University has provided virtual classrooms using a combination of e-mail and MUDDs.
http://www.csu.edu.au/research/cstl/oztl_net/

There is also an excellent Australian e-mail newsletter devoted to online learning: The ONLINE-ED newsletter.
http://www.edfac.unimelb.edu.au/online-ed/

Prime Characteristics

While there are quite a few attempts to exploit Web-based strategies for adult learning, many of these are poorly disguised old ventures dressed up for the Internet. In order to distinguish between the more promising and the least valuable of these efforts, it pays to apply criteria that filter out the tired old models in favor of dynamic new designs.

Online Learning

• Modules

Online learning relies upon modules to provide "chunks" of learning that eventually fit together into a comprehensive and coherent whole. The modules work a bit like LEGO blocks, connecting and interlocking as the learner "constructs" a new skill and knowledge base.

Modules work especially well because they offer the busy adult an opportunity to pick up new ideas and competencies in "bite size" pieces well suited to the highly pressurized life styles of most teachers.

In many instances, modules can stand on their own. In some cases, as when skills must be built upon prior skills, a particular sequence of modules may be required.

• Linked Resources

Thanks to the Web and other networked electronic resources, the developer of online modules can quite easily enrich the learning by linking participants to great treasures. The older technologies, because they often relied on physical objects, were necessarily less generous in their offerings.

• Exploration

Formal classrooms allowed for little exploration. Our teachers often did the sorting, sifting and selecting for us. Information was delivered already packaged like processed cheese.

Online experiences encourage the learner to roll up sleeves and get messy. The theory is that knowledge sticks when the learner is able to delve fully into the material.

Curiosity and great questions drive exploration. The better the questions . . . the deeper and more engaging the exploration. The basic goal is to make sense of the most important concepts and generalizations, to "chew" on these new understandings until the learner can "digest" them.

• Purpose

The purpose of online learning should be clearly stated up front.

Online Learning

It is not "seat time." In most cases online learning is meant to equip the participant with skills, attitudes and new understandings, all of which may be measured.

• Journey

The journey metaphor captures the dominant theme of independence and choice. While the destination may be chosen for us, the best online learning allows us considerable choice regarding the path we may follow.

The route may wander and weave about as much as a river meandering through a delta, seemingly lost but intent upon reaching the sea. Learning of simple skills may be structured, but the development of conceptual understanding often requires a less linear route.

Advantages

Online learning has dramatic advantages over the delivery systems that we have tried and found lacking in the past.

• Learning vs. Teaching

The prevalent emphasis upon teaching will shift to learning. We will have less "sage on the stage" and more "guide on the side." Online learning is especially suited to this shift, as control passes from teacher to learner. No more "leave the driving to us." It's time to take the wheel and the gearshift firmly in hand. Time to steer our own path, teaching ourselves as we move on down the road.

• Independent of Time & Place

For too many years many folks have acted as if all learning must occur within a rectangular space with rows of seats or tables. We are beginning to see new delivery systems that are much less dependent upon formal schedules and spaces. The classroom may occupy less and less of our time during the next century. Learning takes place in our minds, not in classrooms, and our minds can perform this work in many different locations . . . whether it be alongside a stream, in a museum, or online.

This is welcome news to teachers who find they have little "wiggle room" in their busy lives to travel an hour each evening to sit in some brick building.

• Self-Paced

The learner decides just how fast to proceed and what route to take toward competency. There are many choices and little outside pressure. Online learning puts responsibility on the learner. Ready to sprint? Then sprint. Eager to stroll? Then stroll.

• Customized

Given the richness of offerings made possible with online learning, each learner can build an experience to match preferences and appetites. The availability of Web resources vastly increases the options available as learners may take Web excursions to enjoy paintings or photographs or electronic books from some of the great museums, libraries, archives and collections of the world.

• Competency-Based

What matters is skill and understanding. One moves forward on the journey when able to prove competency or knowledge. Check points along the path require periodic demonstration of ability before movement is permitted. As part of this approach, no one is required to waste time on topics, skills or concepts previously mastered.

• No Heroes

Online learning can produce great results without heroic staff developers, charismatic presenters or especially talented trainers. Properly designed, these experiences allow for a high degree of independence. While the learning is often well served by dialogue, no teacher or leader need be present. Quality results are achieved without the tremendous expense associated with "train the trainer" models.

Online Learning

• Uniform

Even though online learning provides many more choices for learners, they may also deliver a uniform level of quality control through the assessment measures built into the journey. No one moves forward unless they can show they have attained a solid level of mastery.

• Cost Effective

While launching the original version of an online learning offering may prove somewhat costly, the price per participant declines rapidly as more and more participants are allowed to move through the lessons without the need of further lesson development and with little need for costly instructors. There will certainly still be tutors and teachers, but they will be playing more of a guiding and supporting role than previously.

Chapter 12 - Coaching for a Change

Coaching may be the most effective way to convert reluctant colleagues into enthusiastic users of new technologies.

As mentioned throughout this book, in the first twenty years of introducing computers to schools, we relied too heavily on staff development classes to introduce computers. These strategies, if we were lucky and talented, sometimes reached an enthusiastic 15-30 per cent of our colleagues. But now we need to reach the perennially reluctant and those who have been eager but frustrated. In order to extend our reach so that nearly all teachers are participating, the times require quite different strategies.

Programs that emphasize coaching and mentor relationships encourage the growth of technology enthusiasts while also supporting and enlisting teachers who have previously been thought reluctant, resistant and technology challenged.

The secret behind this method is the customization made possible when a coach or mentor works alongside one or more colleagues. The learning opportunities are matched to the readiness level, skills and preferences of each teacher. The content is drawn from the actual curriculum. The experience is fully integrated into classroom life and expressly designed to produce student learning. Technologies are infused in ways that support teacher goals. There is nothing diversionary or disruptive about the time investment.

Technology Coaching Programs

To launch a coaching program, a district sets aside funding for full time staff positions that are meant to last anywhere from 3-5 years. Each coach can team with 20-35 teachers per year in projects that last anywhere from one to two weeks.

The goal is to reach every teacher within a 3-5 year time period in a succession of waves.

Each project begins with planning sessions during which the coach and the partner identify a chunk of curriculum that might be well served by the introduction of electronic technologies. The coach and the teacher then develop and implement a unit plan to implement and test as a team.

Elements of Success

According to the research of Bruce Joyce and Beverly Showers, when compared to other adult learning strategies, peer coaching has the greatest chance of changing teacher behaviors. At the same time, we have learned that some coaching and mentor programs work better than others. Factors associated with success include the following:

• Effective Mentors

The best coaches put their partners at ease. While it is tempting to hire impressively advanced technology pioneers as coaches, the most important criteria have to do with the diplomacy, tact and relationship building necessary to win the confidence and trust of partners. We need to be cautious about promoting teachers whose superior performance and attitudes might actually hamper their effectiveness with peers.

• Planning

Coaching must engage both the coach and the partner in planning for technology use. It is not uncommon for classroom teachers to view the coach as someone to teach technology to the students. Instead of participating as full partners in the design and delivery of technology rich lessons, they might prefer to sit at the back of the room correcting papers while the coach offers a welcome respite from the normal teaching routine. It must be clear from the very beginning that the classroom teacher remains the teacher.

Coaching for a Change

• Job Description

Coaches do best when their role is clearly defined on a single page that can be handed to partners and others such as the building principal. If coaching is new to a district, there will be many misunderstandings regarding the purpose of the program. A clear job description can help by mapping out just what the coach does. And just what the partner does. This job description becomes an important tool to assist with the development of a new working relationship.

• Teaming

Coaches are not substitutes. They are partners. Both the coach and the partner must feel shared responsibility for the technology infused lessons. Both participate in the development and the testing of lessons. Both invent. Both teach.

• Respect

Coaches must be cautious about attitude. Many teachers who do not make much use of electronic tools are extraordinarily effective and talented professionals. If coaches view their role as correcting deficiencies, the chances of creating trusting partnerships are remote.

• Time

Joint time to invent technology rich units increases shared ownership of innovations. For each week long unit to be developed and implemented, the coach and the partner will need as much as a day away from pressing classroom demands to work on the lesson planning. Without the provision of joint planning time, it is tempting for the coach to step in with lessons created without the partner's engagement.

• Clear Expectations

Growth is most likely to be widespread when everyone is expected to participate without exception. The district clarifies technology expectations for each level in curriculum guides and all teachers are given 2-3 years to develop the ability to translate those expectations into classroom realities. Commitment to this learning process is formalized in annual professional growth plans, that are shared between principals and teachers. The question is not whether a teacher will participate. It is "when" and "how" that becomes the issue.

• Support

The coach contributes encouragement as well as knowledge to help the partner find new ways to achieve success in the classroom. The partner contributes curriculum savvy and experience to guide the invention process. This is a case of mutual support as two professionals consider the best ways to blend new technologies into classroom life.

• Customization

The best results emerge when the experience is well matched to the partner's style and characteristics. This is not about showing teachers to teach the way the coach would teach. The coach empowers the partner to make use of technologies in ways that dovetail with the partner's teaching style. At the same time, we would hope that these technologies might allow many teachers to broaden their repertoire and expand their range of styles. Those who have relied mostly on direct instruction may come to value the student learning that can result when students are required to do more of the work.

• Deliverance

The ultimate goal is to pass the responsibility for continued success to the partner. This coaching experience should be viewed as an interim measure to support program development, with the coach disengaging and moving on to work with others. The partner carries on and extends the newly acquired strategies to other units and other lessons. If the coach returns in a few months or the following year, it is not to "repeat the technology unit." The next round of visits prompts the development of a new unit.

Coaching for a Change

• Assessment

More growth occurs when there is a system to track and recognize change. In many places, failure to collect evidence of change can contribute to uneven implementation and can result in "virtual change." The reporting system may be as simple as a monthly note to the principal indicating when and how teachers are carrying out the technology expectations written into the curriculum guides.

Challenges & Frustrations

Despite the strong case that can be made for peer coaching, coaches and mentors frequently report surprising levels of resistance. It takes considerable talent, persistence and tact to steer over, around and through the many obstacles that may arise whenever one teacher in a system is offered as a resource to support the growth in teaching of another. While these obstacles rarely surface in a public manner, they can swiftly negate the influence of a coaching program that ignores them.

• Privacy Concerns

Some people love the privacy that accompanies the job of teaching. You enter your classroom, shut the door and rarely see another adult enter. While some teachers welcome visits, partners and team opportunities, others prize their separation and their privacy. They do not welcome other teachers within their domain.

• Equal Unequals

In many schools there is a pecking order that may have nothing to do with teaching skill. When one teacher is designated as especially talented in some respect, it may turn power relationships upside down, setting conflicts in motion that may undermine the value of the coaching. If the coach is younger and highly talented, he or she may be taught a few lessons about power. The intended recipient of support may resent the implication that help is needed and may punish the coach for violating the established order.

• Ego Needs

Some folks have invested decades in the creation of master teacher images that they are usually reluctant to set aside for any reason. While many of us see continued learning and reflective practice as a sign of a masterful teacher, some equate this process with disrobing and dismemberment. They may resist coaching because it represents an "unmasking" that threatens ego.

• Comfort Zone

Learning almost always involves discomfort, and yet there are those working in schools who seek to minimize discomfort by keeping life moving along as smoothly as possible. Because a good coach will nearly always ask partners to venture out of their comfort zones into new territory, their offers of support may be seen as threatening rather than reassuring.

Coaches Coaching Coaches

The best coaching programs will provide district coaches with many opportunities to step back as a team to consider the change process. Which strategies are working? How does the program need to be changed? Which strategies should be discarded? What are the best ways to involve principals? What new discoveries need to be blended into the original model?

Frequent gatherings of coaches are essential because they are one of the best ways to overcome the obstacles mentioned in the second part of this chapter.

Chapter 13 - Creating a Vanguard

The better the job we do of identifying, grooming and rewarding local talent, the greater the professional growth and development we will see. It is a simple (but usually ignored) truth. We are too often penny wise and people foolish.

Change takes root when grown from local seeds planted by those who know the soil, the sky and the prevailing winds. Programs and strategies grown elsewhere usually flounder and founder.

Home grown. Home made. Home cooked. Innovation thrives when you find and encourage the right people. They return the favor by customizing and adjusting programs to match local needs, local people and local conditions.

Talent. Inventiveness. An almost cussed irreverence for the way things are spozed to be . . . Be on the lookout for talent. Find it. Grow it. Encourage it. We can never have enough.

Identifying Talent

Think big. Your goal is to find and encourage no fewer than ten per cent of the district teaching staff to become technologically savvy trend setters, pioneers and leaders. These are the folks who will steer the invention of your program and will build enticing professional development opportunities for their colleagues.

Don't go out and pick the obvious people. No more same-old, same-old. We are looking to change the mix dramatically. We are looking for all different learning styles and personality traits as well as representation from all the various factions and groups that are typical in most school districts.

We don't want plain old pea soup. We crave five alarm, eight bean chili. The individuals don't all need to be five alarm. It's the combination that makes for hot and spicy chemistry.

At least half of this **vanguard** should be people who nobody would ever expect to see leading any technology efforts. That's the beauty of the strategy. We jump right out of the rut. We are suddenly driving "off road" with plenty of flair and passion.

"I can't believe Anthony is up there showing us all these fantastic new tricks. I thought he hated technology?"

We seek five essential traits and will cultivate the sixth . . .

1. Nerve

"That Anthony sure has a lot of nerve!"

All members of this cadre must be able to question the unquestionable and challenge the way things have always happened in the past. Each "recruit" must possess a "can do" attitude. A strong forward lean. The flexibility to test out a whole bunch of possibilities. A willingness to trip, stumble and fall into excellence.

Folks with **nerve** are not always easy . . .

2. Talent

They must be very, very good at something in their lives outside of school, but it need not be related to technology at the outset. What we seek here is the capacity to stand out and be exceptional . . . the passion to excel, to push the limits.

We ultimately expect to harness the intensity they have shown for cooking, dancing, painting, gardening, fly-fishing, constructing or whatever in the service of our technology initiative.

3. Respect

No pariahs, no castoffs, no outcasts and no [serious] troublemakers. They must all be viewed with considerable respect by their peers. Not necessarily well loved, but well respected, at least.

4. Empathy

All members of the vanguard must have strong empathy for colleagues and the disparate frustrations, rewards and challenges that typify the work lives of teachers.

Each person must be caring as well as capable of working toward accord and harmony.

5. Balance

Each person must add to the overall balance of the vanguard, offering offsetting qualities, tendencies and preferences that are reflective of the larger professional community's diversity.

To be cultivated . . .

6. Eagerness

A passionate love for new technologies is not a necessary "starting trait." If we do a good job of encouraging and grooming the vanguard, we should be able to inspire the eagerness we seek.

In contrast to those who have always been excited about technology, the teacher who has been recently "converted" may achieve a special level of credibility from peers.

Who does the selecting?

Each district must follow its own traditions when developing local talent, but the best approach probably intermixes a number of strategies. A designated leader in the technology area may do much of the selecting. Technology teams at the site level may play a major role. And self selection in response to advertised opportunities may round out the process.

Creating a Vanguard

Grooming and Encouraging

What do we do with these people? This vanguard?

We provide an incredibly rich menu of learning opportunities that will cause growth spurts and bursts. We seek more than increased skill levels. This is not just about knowledge. We are hoping for a major increase of the group's imaginative and innovative spirit.

We are looking for experiences that will feed their creative instincts and nurture their spirits.

> The (person) with a new idea is a crank until the idea succeeds.
>
> Mark Twain

Excursions - Take Me Away!

Schools and school districts are (in most cases) remarkably confining. To provoke new thinking and inspire new possibilities, we must send teachers across borders and boundaries.

Most districts limit travel. We need to radically expand the travel opportunities of our vanguard so they can escape (and learn to challenge) the boxes and traditions they work within.

1. School-to-Work

Every member of the vanguard visits 2-3 technology rich workplaces annually to witness how information technologies may transform decision-making and problem-solving. Visits should include the not-for-profit sector. These visits lift their eyes beyond the horizon. "How do we give our students a taste of this world outside? How do we prepare them?"

Creating a Vanguard

2. Outstanding/Outlier/Anomaly Schools

We are looking for programs, teachers, students and classrooms that have "deviated or departed" from the normal way of doing business (but with some success). These may, at first seem "peculiar, irregular, or abnormal" in some ways (**American Heritage Dictionary**). All the better!

Good time to hop on an airplane or a ferry. Too many visits take place within the same state or county. There are only a handful of states that have done much with networked technologies in schools. Even if you live in one of those states, you should be visiting the other 6-10 who are doing something worthwhile.

In all too many cases, schools twist new technologies to perform old tasks. Visits to "mainstream" programs may do more damage than good. In two decades of using computers, they have remained, according to many studies, peripheral to the regular program.

We are seeking models where the technologies have become fully integrated tools supporting powerful student thought and invention. But beware of marketing and PR efforts. You cannot judge a school by its Web site!

3. Great Gatherings

We send members of the vanguard to join groups of other inventive souls who are trying to create the future, using whatever tools and inspiration they can find, whether it be research, exploration, discussion, speculation, metaphysical inquiry, or scientific inquiry. The important ingredients are inquiring minds and ample curiosities.

Oddly, educational conferences and workshops (even those devoted to new technologies) may not always be the best source of inspiration. The institutional pressures to maintain tradition can undermine the innovative potential of such events. Same-old, same-old can prevail over dramatic change.

Seek out unusual gatherings sponsored by the World Future

Creating a Vanguard

Society http://www.wfs.org/wfs/, Internet World http://
events.Internet.com/ , the Participatory Design Conference sponsored
by the Computer Professionals for Social Responsibility http://
www.cpsr.org/conferences/pdc98/index.html or The National Center
for Urban Partnerships http://www.ncup.org/.

Some of the best experiences will occur outside the official
proceedings as members of the vanguard swap ideas, questions and
insights with other attendees.

The Club House - The Play's the Thing

Some of the best new ideas occur in the tree house. It's not the
elevation . . . it's the company . . . the playful and foolish atmosphere.

Teaching being a profession that isolates adults one from another
for the most part, we need to create gathering places and rituals so that
the vanguard can enjoy the fruits of synergy. Perhaps we take turns
inviting colleagues to our homes for coffee or wine. Or maybe we
find a coffee shop downtown that offers strong brew.

The important thing is getting away from the ho-hum drum of
regular school meetings and meeting spaces. If we expect people to
take flight, we need to get them together where their ideas can flow
and percolate, roll over and boil. Synergy (the chemistry of good
minds joined in chewing upon a challenge) responds to good surround-
ings, good company and good coffee.

Flights of Fancy - Imagine That!

Every member of this vanguard should have a substantial budget
to support the purchase of books, the use of electronic resources and
the payment for subscriptions of various kinds. $400-$500 can make a
very large impact upon the information resources available to fuel
each person's imagination.

With the advent of "push technology" teachers can sign up for all
manner of information "alerts" that are customized to match their

interests and arrive daily or weekly in their e-mail baskets. Some are free - like listservs. DejaNews provides a good search mechanism to locate listservs and newsgroups. (http://www.dejanews.com/) - while others cost money (NewsHound's customized news alert and retrieval service, available on the World Wide Web at http://www.newshound.com.

The investment of each dollar in good information for members of the vanguard will pay tenfold in flights of imagination.

To Build a Fire - The Inventor's Workshop

Little funding is available in most school districts for folks to gather together for the actual construction process. Professional development is often viewed as training, not building. As outlined in the chapter on invention, it turns out that the process of invention actually motivates more learning of technology skills and greater integration into regular classrooms.

Home grown. Home made. Home cooked. Innovation thrives when you find and encourage the right people.

Nobody's Fool- The Power of Mentoring

We plan so our vanguard may meet with sages and seers from nearby and far away. We expect that they will, in turn, provide support and guidance for the learning journeys of their peers.

The challenge is finding someone worth questioning. For every dozen so-called "experts" and consultants there may be one soothsayer. We need to be cautious of those who label themselves as gurus or futurists.

Before someone might qualify as a mentor or TEACHER to our vanguard, we would hope their ideas, theories and suggestions were tested in the classroom, their wisdom won through experience. There are far too many glib technologists propounding marketing and testifying. They market a bandwagon without axles, yoke, wheels or oxen.

Creating a Vanguard

We ask three simple questions:

• What work are you doing with teachers and students to see which strategies actually make a difference?
• What have you invented?
• Where have you failed?

If they haven't failed, chances are they haven't taken risks, created real programs or learned much worth sharing.

We meet with outsiders because we hope to learn from their mistakes as well as their victories and successes. We hope they will help us steer by the stars as well as some chart or compass. We expect that they will not insult us with simple answers and prescriptions and recipes.

We yearn for the thinker who knows that the questions are more important than the answers. Questions give us power. Answers rarely match local conditions and circumstances.

Within our own districts, the power of mentoring is immense. Peer-to-peer, we see teachers extending a helping hand, an encouraging word. First one leads. Then they trade places. Each possesses a special expertise. No hierarchy here. Mentoring can be a movable feast.

Issues of Cost

Many of the suggestions offered in this chapter cost money, some will complain, but the most costly mistake of all is failing to develop the "human infrastructure" adequately so a district invests millions of dollars in networking and equipment that is shunned.

Rather than penny wise and people foolish, reserve 25 per cent or more of your hardware investment for adult learning. You are better off with fewer computers used actively than many computers sleeping through the day underutilized.

Conclusion

We don't want plain old pea soup. We crave five alarm, eight bean chili. If we expect to see our students and our teachers leaning over monitor screens, intently exploring rich information with powerful tools, we must encourage local talent and invest mightily in providing opportunities for growth.

Chapter 14 - Reaching the Reluctants

Sally Jane sits at her desk peering past rows of empty student desks toward three silent computers grouped at the back of her classroom. It is the third week of school, but these computers have yet to be turned on.

Sally Jane is a technology reluctant. Although she has been teaching as long as computers have been known to schools, she has resisted their use while concentrating instead upon good teaching. Her students love her. She is demanding, sometimes inspiring, and is known within her community for improving student performance, but Sally Jane has not yet seen much value in two decades of technology promises and products. She is reluctant to fix her class if it isn't broken.

****

Even as schools are busily filling classrooms with computers, a large percentage of teachers remain reluctant and skeptical. Unfortunately, much of the technology professional development of the past two decades was designed by technology enthusiasts with little empathy for reluctants. They have failed to convert reluctance into enthusiasm. They have failed to address the very real concerns of reluctants.

This chapter argues that technology reluctants have special needs, interests and learning styles that must be addressed with respect and ingenuity if we expect to see such teachers embrace the new technologies being placed in their classrooms.

Reaching the Reluctants

Little has been done to prepare reluctant technology users for the networked computers flooding into their rooms.

We have evidence (Becker, 1999) that as many as seventy per cent of the teachers in American schools fall into the "reluctant" or "late adopter" categories when it comes to computers and other new technologies. Some fall into these categories because they have been given little support, few opportunities and marginal equipment. Others, like Sally Jane, may knowingly resist.

A 1995 report from the Office of Technology Assessment, **Making the Connection**, (ftp://gandalf.isu.edu/pub/ota/teachers.tech/01readme.txt) estimated that less than a quarter of our teachers had managed to integrate these tools into regular classroom programs.

In addition, the annual **Technology in Education 1998 Report** from Market Data Retrieval reports that Internet access has increased dramatically while just seven percent of schools claim that the majority of their teachers are at an Advanced skill level (able to integrate technology use into the curriculum). (http://www.schooldata.com)

The CEO Forum School Technology and Readiness Report (Year Two) states that "Only 20% of teachers report feeling very well prepared to integrate educational technology into classroom instruction."

The characteristics of late adopters are profoundly different from those of early adopters.

Late adopters are teachers who have not yet embraced new technologies and have not yet blended these tools into their daily classroom learning activities. The term originated in the technology marketplace outside of schools as a way to differentiate between early and late buyers of new technologies.

Crossing the Chasm (Moore, 1991) describes the huge "gap" or "chasm" between these two groups and suggests that many technology companies failed to survive because they assumed that technology

adoption (and sales) would be a smooth progression from early enthusiasts into highly profitable later markets and customers. The assumption that late adopters follow the lead of early adopters has proven to
be wrong-minded and dangerous, according to Moore. Crossing the
chasm between these groups, states Moore, requires a mammoth
campaign that includes special attention to the vastly different needs,
perspectives and demands of the late adopters. What works for pioneers does not work for the later group.

This insight has virtually escaped the notice of the educational
world. And networking has virtually removed the notion of teachers
as customers with choices. They awaken one day with computers in
their rooms without having requested them.

• Late adopters want proof of results before they buy.

One of the most important differences Moore identifies between
the two groups is the expectation of late adopters that new technologies must make a very big difference in outcomes and performance.
They have little tolerance for change and are unwilling to shift time
tested behaviors unless there is compelling evidence that the investment of time and effort will pay big dividends.

• Late adopters want a complete, finished product before they buy.

They also expect a complete package, a total solution that is user
friendly, complete and well supported. They are, in Moore's terms,
pragmatists. They are conservative and distrustful of change for
change sake. They have their eye on the bottom line. They have no
patience for half-baked ideas, unproven technologies and untested
schemes.

Ignoring the chasm is a recipe for failure.

Even though Moore's work was based on corporate customers, his
observations speak directly to the widening chasm within the educa-

tional world as schools rush to network and place computers in every classroom regardless of teacher "buy-in."

Too many districts put the network "cart" ahead of the learning "horse," as wiring, cabling and hardware purchases race far ahead of program development and human resource development.

Schools have bought half a product - infrastructure without compelling curriculum value. They have hooked up to the Internet as if it were some magnificent "digital library" instead of an "information yard-sale."

Ignoring legitimate curriculum questions while skimping on professional development investments is dangerous. The two are interwoven. Unless we clarify how these networks might improve the reading, writing and reasoning of students, we will face large numbers of teachers questioning the value of the new "toys."

Strategies to Reach Late Adopters and Reluctant Technology Users

Schools must pay particular attention to the needs and interests of reluctant technology users. This group will require a sustained three year commitment of 15-60 hours annually of adult learning experiences tailored to special attitudes and preferences.

Guidelines for reaching the reluctant teacher:

1. Clarify the bottom line: gains in student performance.

Most reluctants have trouble relating to the inflated rhetoric of technology enthusiasts. They want to know that their work will result in higher test scores and better performance as measured by increasingly demanding state tests. They want to hear about the "bottom line." And yet no one is providing evidence of such gains. To win the reluctants, we must show measurable results. They are not won over by talk of multimedia or fanciful virtual bike trips across Africa.

130

2. Deliver a complete package.

Most learning opportunities associated with networks require a high degree of inventiveness. Conservative teachers are looking for excellent packages that have been tested, refined and perfected. They don't have time to "mess around." We need to offer more than cables and computers. Strong learning models such as **WebQuest** (http://edweb.sdsu.edu/webquest/webquest.html) are persuasive when introducing reluctant teachers to networks.

3. Eliminate risk and surprise.

Generally speaking, reluctants do not enjoy surprises, disappointments and adventures, especially when they happen during class time. They may sign up for white water rafting outside of school, but they would never select it as a model of instruction. We must supply them with experiences requiring little risk.

4. Speak their language.

Many technology proponents speak a language guaranteed to alienate the reluctants. They act as if everything from the past (like lecturing) is bad while any new, technology-rich experience (like surfing) is good. They use terms like "constructivist learning" and "student centered classrooms." Reluctants view this rhetoric with great suspicion. They pride themselves on demanding serious, rigorous learning from students, steering clear of fads and fashions.

5. Offer continual support.

Ongoing support is more important than classes and training. The emotional dimensions of this challenge keep many reluctants from stepping into the technology game. They see networks crashing. They need the technology to work reliably, and they want someone by their side when anything goes wrong.

6. Emphasize teams.

Some of the most impressive gains take place when teachers elect to work in small groups of mixed abilities and styles. The reluctant may be won over by the impressive discoveries realized while exploring with a group of peers, some of whom are more comfortable with mice.

7. Find out what turns them on.

The most change occurs when someone "buys in." They are most apt to "buy in" when their personal passions and interests are at stake. "What's in it for me?" In all too many districts no one ever asks. There is too little time spent figuring out what turns people on to learning new tools. Wise districts periodically ask teachers of all types what issues are most important to them and how they prefer to learn. Example: "Technology in my Life Survey" - http://fromnowon.org/ techlife.html

8. Provide rewards and incentives.

"What's in it for me?" Too little attention is paid to motivation. How can a district spend $ 20,000,000 on computers while begrudging teachers basic incentives to learn and use the new technologies? In too many places teachers are expected to donate their own afternoons, evenings and weekends to the learning of new tools. This is serious work deserving full compensation and plenty of recognition.

9. Don't rely on pioneers alone to plan for reluctants.

Pioneers rarely sympathize with reluctants or understand their issues. Pioneers have different needs and far more tolerance for frustration. They rarely understand reluctants or how they learn. They find it difficult to design professional development for reluctants that works.

Online References

Technology in Education 1998 Report from Market Data Retrieval
http://www.schooldata.com

Reaching the Reluctants

The CEO Forum School Technology and Readiness Report (Year Two) **http://www.ceoforum.org/**

Chapter 15 - Planning for Success

Too much professional development is done on the fly, haphazardly and absentmindedly. Too many schools rely upon time-honored but discredited "training" models. If we expect to see a return on our technology investments, sound program planning is a must. Professional development must incorporate what we have learned about best practice.

Effective Program Design

We know that the most effective programs provide for the following:

- The varied developmental stages of learners
- The diverse learning styles of participants
- An abundant mix of opportunities and choices
- A long range view
- Personal planning commitments
- Motivation

What would happen if we advertised a rich and varied menu of adult learning opportunities? Not just classes after school. No disappointing little brochure of tired programs. No "Introduction to Microsoft Word." How about providing a hundred or more adventures and choices instead? Enticing. Irresistible.

We launch a Pro-D (professional development) design team. We engage members of the district technology cadre or vanguard. We select those who are innovative, questioning and aware of diverse needs. We make sure they all have a clear sense of what we mean by adult learning.

We give this design team the challenge of creating a hundred selections for the first year and a hundred more for each of the next four years.

Picture a 100 cell planning grid. Fill each cell with a learning option. Mix it up. Make them different. Only 25 per cent should be classes of various kinds. The rest should be a mixture of visits and excursions, informal contacts and study groups as well as readings, explorations and support groups.

Planning Grid for Year One
(Make large enough to fill a conference room wall)

Some activities should be very challenging. Others introductory. Design some for the wild and crazy pioneers. Develop others for the sages and reluctants. Consider and address all learning styles. How many different kinds of salsa can you invent and serve? Mild, medium and HOT! Plain tomato and cucumber. Fried green tomato, cilantro and black bean . .

Types of Offerings

Schools are finding that sometimes the greatest growth in technology skill, comfort and usage occurs when teachers can count upon informal support and timely exchanges. An effective Pro-D program combines these kinds of small group, personal opportunities with more traditional offerings.

Classes

Long the staple of district programs, classes will remain an important element, but we will see a major shift toward offerings that emphasize teaching and learning strategies instead of software programs. Teachers will learn how to teach technology enhanced social studies, art and science classes. For example, they will sign up for a course on "crunching population statistics" and learn how to ask questions of vast databases using tools like spreadsheets with charting functions.

Software applications will be included only to the extent they are actually needed to support the learning tasks. We will see less direct instruction with a teacher leading a class through a series of steps. This approach will be replaced by hands-on explorations. The instructor will serve as "guide on the side."

Teachers will often work as teams to solve learning challenges. Frequently they will share screens and work with considerable team independence. They will enjoy the *Engaged Learning* strategies we hope to see them turn and offer to their students.

Study Groups and Tutorials

Many teachers say they prefer learning new programs in small groups. When polling audiences, I have found that small group tutorials are the dominant preference over structured classes every time. And this leaning is shared by teachers in every Canadian and Australian audiences I have questioned.

Districts should heed the research of Bruce Joyce, who recommends that every teacher join a team of 3-4 colleagues meeting weekly to plan and enjoy professional growth throughout the year.

(Joyce, 1990). Changing school culture through staff development. Alexandria, VA: ASCD. http://www.ascd.org/services/eric/staff2.html

Following Joyce's model, teachers run their own show to a great extent. When they wish assistance, they call upon colleagues and district resources to supplement their own efforts. One or more of the 3-4 annual target areas might include the challenge of enhancing classroom learning with information technologies.

Planning for Success

Visits & Excursions

Dramatic transformations in behavior and attitude can result from changes of location and shifts in perspective. Visits to information rich work places may deepen teachers' understanding of the need to equip students with 21st Century skills. But the range of visits and excursion should extend further. Teachers frequently work in isolation from adult society and have few chances to observe how new tools are modifying the ways people communicate, share, invent and produce goods.

Invention & Lesson Development

Even when teachers are blessed with rich Pro-D offerings, they are rarely afforded the time to translate theory into practice. When they can create lesson plans and unit plans, we begin to see an impact on the daily events of classrooms.

"This was so much better than staff development!" enthused one group of Texas teachers from the Grand Prairie ISD after spending a day constructing online, Web-based research modules for students. http://www.gpisd.org/gpisd/departments/c_and_i/inst_tech/modules/ modulepage.html

This inventing and lesson development is so important districts should allocate 50 per cent of their Pro-D time to support real program integration.

Informal Contacts

Many staff report that one-on-one exchanges prove extremely beneficial. Provided there is trust, the support of a more advanced partner can stimulate "leapfrogging" past obstacles and barriers.

"The best way to win widespread use of new technologies is to provide **just-in-time support** . . . assistance and encouragement when needed. Not tomorrow. Not next week. Now!"

By making sure a major portion of the staff possesses special technology skills, we create a culture of support, meaning that every teacher can count on finding assistance in a matter of minutes.

While few consider these support structures to be "professional development," they enable faculty to advance when it comes to technology usage and integration.

Readings & Explorations

Too little support is provided for reading. If every teacher could count on a professional book and journal budget of $200 yearly, the district would reap several thousand dollars worth of learning. In the same manner, dial-in access to electronic resources can pay great dividends during hours at home and away from school. Too often, the focus on seat time and classes has blinded districts to the alternatives.

Independent Learning

Many teachers report that they taught themselves the last software program they learned. Why not do a better job of acknowledging and encouraging such efforts? Even though *Microsoft* permits a free home copy of office software, how many districts actively support this benefit or provide resources such as books and videos to help the independent learner?

The Crucial Role of Assessment

As outlined in a preceding chapter, a commitment to assessment helps us to steer our professional development efforts forward.

With a reasonable investment of time and money, we can learn a good deal about our colleagues and their responses to our professional development offerings. The better job we do of assessing, the better the match between program and participant. We use what we learn to enrich, enhance and upgrade our offerings.

Planning for Success

Keeping an Eye on the Horizon

Technologies are changing at such a rapid pace that we must guard against complacency and routines. The Pro-D design team must peer around Time's corner to see what is coming next. How will search engines change? How will periodical collections change? How important will Intranets become? What new forms of adult learning are evolving?

Charged with the design and development of a five-year program, the team weeds out yesterday's fading offerings while inventing a whole new generation of possibilities.

Personal Planning Commitments

To make this kind of planning succeed, we ask that each teacher formally accept responsibility for professional growth. Each individual maps out a five-year personal journey, taking advantage of the rich offerings made available by the district. All staff members are expected to make the journey toward powerful use of technology for student learning, but each may select a path well suited to their own special needs and passions.

Chapter 16 - Study Groups

It is early Thursday morning and the school parking lot is dark and empty. A good hour before most teachers will drive into the lot, a battered Volvo, a Ford pick-up and a highly polished, gleaming black Chrysler convertible wheel into reserved spots.

Grumbling about the early hour while clutching Big Gulps or Starbucks Venti Cups, four teachers emerge from the three cars and find their way down darkened hallways to the school's media center where they can turn on the lights and resume the electronic research they have been pursuing for several weeks.

Middle school teachers all, they are using the network to study breast cancer. Each is a cancer patient or the relative of a cancer patient. They are developing information literacy skills while investigating an issue of personal urgency.

Study groups may be one of the best ways to create the Mega Change called for by networking schools. We are finding that informal models such as study groups inspire the most impressive growth. Teachers appreciate the opportunity to explore new technologies with partners of their own choosing. They respond best to frequent, sustained support tailored to their personal preferences. They welcome the chance to partner with colleagues as they invent technology-infused lessons for their students.

Unlike the technology coaching strategy outlined in a previous chapter, study groups are flat and non-hierarchical. Groups may call upon experts when they want them, but much of the time teachers are learning with relatively equal partners.

Study Groups

Characteristics of Effective Study Groups

For this strategy to work, it is best if the entire faculty of a school signs up. Every teacher makes a commitment to continued professional growth and joins with a study group of like-minded colleagues who will create a journey of self-discovery.

Teams of 3-4 teachers
There is no magical number, but a group of 3-4 participants allows for the right amount of dialogue and participation. One of the goals is to establish balanced and vigorous participation by all. As groups climb above 4 members, this goal becomes increasingly difficult to attain.

Clear learning goals
Each team identifies 3-4 topics, concerns or concepts they wish to explore. Some of these should be related to school goals and student achievement while others may be more personally related to the shared interests and needs of team members. These goals should be specified in writing as part of a team planning process that is shared with the building principal.

Weekly sessions
The group of adult learners gathers at least once each week for an hour or more. In most cases, the actual timing can be worked out to meet the life style issues and schedules of group members, but many schools have also rearranged schedules to build time into the teacher week when students may be otherwise engaged.

Writing in the Summer, 1997 issue of the **Journal of Staff Development**, Carlene U. Murphy describes "how many schools have carved study time out of their schedules in order to make professional development a seamless part of their daily work." "Finding Time for Faculties to Study Together." http://www.nsdc.org/library/jsd/jsdsm97murp.html

Study Groups

Learning as discovery

This is no packaged tour to the pyramids complete with air conditioned bus and travel guide. Each team must find its own way, create its own itinerary and invent its own path. If all goes well, participants will emerge with benefits they could not have listed at the outset, with outcomes that emerged along the way. Discovery learning is based on the premise that we do not know what we do not know when we start the journey and can only learn what we should know by approaching the experience with an open mind.

Self steering learning path

Because this is a process of discovery, the path of each group may wander a bit like a river reaching toward the sea. While the year may begin with a written plan that seems linear and organized, in many cases, surprises along the way will probably create a serpentine pattern that is evidence that participants are steering their own course and adjusting direction as they acquire new knowledge.

Internal and external resources

Unlike traditional staff development, study groups direct their own learning and often create their own experiences and opportunities, relying upon a mixture of internal and external resources. While they may call upon experts from time to time, the focus is most often upon self reliance and the development of autonomy. The operating presumption is that members can teach themselves much of what needs to be learned. They can also learn at a pace that is often better suited to individual needs and preferences than lessons delivered by so-called experts.

Just in time learning

Study groups set schedules but usually end up breaking them. Once the journey begins, provided it is deeply rooted in the personal passions and curiosities of team members, it is nearly impossible to restrict learning to the times officially designated. Most participants will find that learning spills over into the regular day, that learning cannot be contained, circumscribed or slowed by the formalities of schedules. Team members become omnivores! They move from "just-in-case learning" to "just-in-time learning." They reach out for new skills and new understandings because they need them to finish whatever quest they are engaged in pursuing. They become impatient, demanding and quite dedicated.

Focus on learning

Unlike most technology staff development offerings, study groups are more focussed on student learning than technologies and software. "How can we lift the reading performance of our least successful students? How could mindware programs like *Inspiration* change the way they approach reading?"

Reporting results

Study groups periodically report progress to the building principal, providing a sketch of their work 2-3 times each year and meeting with the principal to discuss ways the principal might provide additional support.

Advantages of Effective Study Groups

While study groups are quite rare in American schools, they offer one of the most promising strategies to induce adult learning. They offer distinct advantages over more traditional approaches . . .

Investment

In all too many cases, staff development has been a ho-hum experience that failed to touch the lives of teachers in ways that might engage them. In contrast, study groups elicit a dramatic level of personal investment as each group is working only on issues and concerns that are central to their careers.

Study Groups

Control

Unlike most staff development, with this model the basic elements of learning are determined by the learners rather than the instructors. This high level of personal control alters the emotional experience in some very positive ways, as learners can seek their way with a reasonable degree of comfort, modifying elements such as pacing to match personal preferences.

Cost

Many schools have been able to free up the time for this kind of adult learning without facing major new expenditures. Note the article by Carleen Murphy identifying strategies to find time.

Support

While traditional staff development for technology has isolated and frustrated large percentages of participants as individuals have struggled with skill agendas put forth by instructors, study groups offer sustained support from team members that is constant and embedded rather than occasional, heroic or sporadic.

Customization

The learning path is customized in ways that courses could not hope to imitate, as each learner has gathered with others of similar interests and styles to explore issues of immense personal importance. Learners are creating their own paths as well as the conditions to accompany learning. They have become their own personal "trainers." They have become instructional designers dedicated to breaking their own path.

Invention

Translation of new possibilities into classroom practice is basic to the model. Study groups are dedicated to classroom action. Participants are intent upon invention and practical results. "How can I do this on Monday morning? How can I use these tools to make my students better readers, better writers and better thinkers."

Conclusion

Study groups provide an effective vehicle to sustain professional development over time. They offer considerable promise, in part, because they place responsibility for directing growth where it belongs. Teachers direct their own journeys. They customize the pathways to match their professional needs and interests.

Chapter 17 - Work Place Visits

We are behind the scenes in Vancouver, British Columbia, wandering through an architectural firm's back office, quizzing the workers and the supervisors in order to find answers to important questions about information, technology and the modern work place.

We notice the low walls of the cubicles, the abundance of personal effects and the informal, job-related talk across walls and corridors. We note a mix of old equipment with brand new. Here and there a monitor rests on a pile of old phone books. We stand impressed before computer-generated visions of a ski village. We see clusters of designers and architects huddled over plans, sharing screens, collaborating and solving problems.

This is professional development?

Meanwhile, spread across the city, a half dozen other teams conduct their own visits, exploring similar questions in as many different settings. One team finds high walls, few personal effects and little informal communication. They jot down findings in small notebooks or laptops. Another team is asking about hiring new employees.

"What traits are you looking for? What background? What computer skills?"

This is professional development?

Come lunch time, we gather back together in a conference room at Simon Fraser University to share findings and discuss the program implications for the West Vancouver Schools.

Workplace Visits

This day of questioning and exploring is a form of professional development consistent with the adult learning principles advocated in previous chapters. Since few classroom teachers have opportunities to see how information and technology may change the modern business or the not-for-profit organization, it is a stretch to develop classroom learning opportunities that provide an appropriate foundation for lifelong learning and employment.

As schools consider the best way to engage teachers in the learning and integrating of new technologies into regular classrooms, work place visits are one of the most persuasive and effective vehicles to promote conviction, understanding and invention. Each teacher should enjoy at least one of these visits as part of their 3-5 year journey of professional development.

The Key Questions

When teams of teachers visit, they act as anthropologists and sociologists. They conduct research . . . trying to understand how life is changing and how they can best prepare their students for such changes. For this reason, the questioning process is paramount. The day begins with an introductory session for all teams to acquaint them with the schedule, the purpose of the day and a suggested list of questions. Each team is then encouraged to expand and adapt this list of questions before heading off to conduct their inquiry.

Process

In what ways can information technologies contribute to (or undermine) an effective flow of work and production?

Competencies

What must people in this environment be capable of doing? What thinking, communicating, persuading and information skills are required for success in this environment?

Traits

What personal qualities and traits (such as curiosity, ingenuity, empathy, originality, persistence, etc.) are desirable or are prized in this culture?

Product

In what ways might information technologies improve the actual quality of this organization's product or services?

Concern

What evidence do you find that information technologies make the organization more or less caring, more or less warm, and more or less humane?

Customization

What evidence do you find that the information technologies make service to clients and/or customers more directly relevant to their needs and particular interests and desires?

Culture

What changes do people report that have resulted from an increasingly technological work place?

Translation

How do any of these findings relate to our work with young people in schools?

Setting Up the Visits

The best outcomes and insights result from visits to a mixture of sites, at least some of which should be filled with surprise. We are taking our colleagues "back stage" to see aspects of business and organizational life they may never see as customers and casual observers. We hope that there will be some startling new insights and some impressive discoveries. We plan by raising the curtain to reveal human stories little understood and little appreciated.

When deciding upon a list of potential sites, look for sites that are in motion, thoroughly committed to change. Make sure to include not-for-profit organizations like universities, museums, hospitals or government agencies as well as businesses. Don't weight your list too heavily with obvious technology companies like IBM, Apple, U.S. West or Motorola – those actually producing the equipment, the software and the infrastructure. The emphasis should be upon companies making use of such products.

All of the sites should be using electronic information technologies in ways that are intended to improve results, but it is not necessary that all be successful or that all serve as models of success. Some of the best lessons can be learned from those who are struggling, disillusioned or frustrated with their new tools.

This raises an important point about visits. Many companies welcome visits by school teachers and are prepared to take you on a guided tour, but that is not exactly what we have in mind here. We are looking beyond the PR message. We hope to delve past the surface and explore the down side of technology along with the benefits.

When you call the public or community relations manager to request the visit, make sure that you share the list of questions and make it clear that you would appreciate if at least half of the time is devoted to the teachers asking questions of the employees. If a company wishes to restrict your contact and questions to the PR manager, you should find a different site to visit.

How big should each team be? More than six creates a burden for the site being visited and restricts the flow of dialogue within the team. Fewer than four limits the energy of the group. As much as possible, try to create an interesting blend within each team. Add a student . . . a parent. Include one teacher from each level of the district . . . an administrator. Mix science and social studies in the same team. Diversity will help to fuel and direct the inquiry process.

Workplace Visits

Discussing the Implications

What did we learn from our visit?

Each team returns for lunch to the conference room where the day began and creates a report for the rest of the groups. First, a team designates a recorder and a reporter. Then the members of the group proceed through the list of questions, taking them one by one, sharing observations, interpretations and inferences until they can build some kind of consensus and synthesize the varying reactions. Sometimes they agree to disagree. Sometimes they include a "minority report."

After an hour of preparation, as the teams are ready to share their findings, a facilitator calls them together, makes sure the chairs are set up in a collaborative,

U-shaped design and proceeds to direct the discussion, going one question at a time.

"We were really surprised," reports one group, "When we asked what computer programs they wanted recruits to know and they said it didn't matter. They want new people to be really good at learning new programs quickly."

"We were really surprised," chimes in another group, "When they kept talking about teams and collaboration and problem-solving. We expected to see more competition and aggressive behavior."

"We were surprised to see old computers and monitors sitting on phone books," adds another.

"But, what did we learn from our visit?"

The facilitator is up front. A recorder sits at a laptop attached to a projector. As the list of discoveries, surprises and implications grows, it appears on the screen at the front of the room. The group can see its work growing and scrolling.

- We need to engage students in more group problem-solving.
- We need to stress more independence and responsibility.
- We should spend less time on software and more time on

learning.
• This is more about information than technology.

Creating Program Change

After all too many technology staff development experiences teachers have learned to complain, "And I shaved my legs for this?" (A line from a Deanna Carter song.)

Work place visits, properly designed, have the power to transcend the ho-hum-drum banalities teachers have learned to expect. They have the power to inspire program change and provide the motivation for integrating information technologies into the daily life of the classroom.

Back stage learning helps teachers see the value of networking. It provides the meaning and the sense of purpose too often missing when folks have rushed to install networks before asking the crucial program questions.

Online References

"Real-World Experiences Can Revitalize Teaching." http://www.nwrel.org/nwreport/dec98/article2.html

This article describes "Teachers Learning in the Community: A Field Guide," the latest offering from the "Connections: Linking Work and Learning" series from the Northwest Regional Laboratory's Education and Work program.

Chapter 18 - Picking Up the Tab

Fresh from a national convention where they witnessed the value of teachers working in teams to invent their own technology rich units, Chris Porter and César Hernandez make an appointment to see their principal.

"We'd like summer money to team with three other science teachers to build a **WebQuest** that matches our middle school science curriculum."

http://edweb.sdsu.edu/webquest/webquest.html

"We think inventing Web-based units is the best way for us to reach every science teacher in the district. If the district funds us, we can mobilize 40 teachers to actually start using all of this equipment we've just seen installed."

The principal smiled, frowned, smiled again, and then pushed back her chair to stand up. A tall woman, she walked over to a window overlooking a courtyard where weeds had long ago choked off any intentional plantings.

"I'd love to help you," she murmured, obviously disturbed. "Your request makes such good sense to me, but I just don't see any money for summer projects. I can't even get them to fix up the courtyard out there . . . "

****

Now that we know networks do little good unless we fund a robust professional development program, how can any "real" district find the money and the time to launch a dynamic effort?

The U.S. Department of Education now recommends that schools should set aside 30 per cent of any technology budget to support professional development. Illinois requires 25 per cent. But few states have similar rules and few districts reach 5 per cent according to a new study for the CEO Forum.

Given the rapid (30-36 month) obsolescence now built into networked PCs, how does any district step off the "replacement treadmill" long enough to fund "human infrastructure?" Don't they have us in a "hardware squeeze?"

This chapter offers a mixture of conventional and unconventional strategies to close the funding gap.

Clarify Purpose

The best way to reserve money for professional development is to clarify educational purpose and spend a smaller share on equipment. The districts with the least control over expenditures and the least investment in pro-D are those who are caught in the trap of trying to maximize the number of PCs in each classroom. This strategy places hardware above all other considerations and rarely results in measurable benefits to students.

One alternative is to place no computers in classrooms without first clarifying how they will serve the programs in those classrooms. If we require that student learning must drive network design, we end up exploring many other delivery systems that can deliver more impact with fewer computers.

Buy Less Stuff

Schools have been buying too much "stuff" and spending too little on the human growth needed to make the investment pay dividends. A district would do better to buy half as many computers while properly funding professional development. 2000 computers used 85 per cent of each day provide more student opportunities than 4000 computers used 20 per cent of each day.

When learning is paramount, we replace the decorating of classrooms with strategic deployment of resources.

Picking Up the Tab

Move Stuff

It turns out that 2-3 computers per class do very little to support integrated technology. Even though it is the favorite deployment model of many networking school districts, 2-3 computers per class fail to provide the "critical mass" required to support an engaged learning program.

Districts can buy half as many computers, put them on wheels and achieve far more student learning by rotating eight computers through a group of four classrooms on a week-by-week schedule. Many schools have found COWS (Computers on Wheels) an excellent way to maximize utilization and student learning while reserving funds to support professional development.

Slow Down Buying Stuff

Another effective strategy is to network fewer classrooms over a longer period of time, making sure that the soil is well cultivated before planting the technology. Instead of putting the "cart before the horse," schools pace the professional development and the equipment installation to maximize results.

Schools should commit to the principle of "no classroom before its time." How can anyone justify placing 3-4 computers in the rooms of teachers who have never embraced the technology? We know that some 60-70% of our teachers are (sensibly) skeptical about the value of all this equipment and the Internet bandwagon. Why not make sure they will welcome (and will use) the equipment before we install it?

If we slow down the installation, we can phase equipment purchases over time and reserve dollars for professional development.

There is no evidence that premature placement of computers accelerates teacher acceptance and use. To the contrary, we have evidence that resistance thrives even in networked classrooms.

Picking Up the Tab

Add Money

Some of us have been arguing for over a decade that technology budgets should include support for all critical elements. Unfortunately, it is rare that budgets provide sufficient funding for professional development, technical staff support or equipment replacement.

Too many districts focus on the acquisition of hardware to launch the network while ignoring the other elements required for success. They strain their budgets trying to push the number of computers per classroom from 2 to 3 or from 4 to 5. There is a disappointing focus on hardware, as if more computers automatically translates into program quality.

Focus Efforts

Dispersing equipment usually dilutes program quality. We can maximize benefits for students by developing "welcoming homes" for networked computers – these would be classrooms of teachers who have teamed to create technology rich learning experiences.

If the social studies department is "gung ho" to proceed but the science department feels reluctant, why not put the equipment where it will find the most use? It is not essential that students have "thin" technology experiences in every program and classroom. If we focus efforts where enthusiasm will translate into program quality, we will do more good for students while reserving funding to support professional development.

Go Casual

Many of the chapters in this book have emphasized that the most dramatic change in teacher behavior may result from the more informal support systems in schools such as study groups and helpful neighbors.

Many of these strategies require more skill than funding. We are talking about the development of collaborative cultures and self-learning teams - inexpensive but complicated to launch and maintain with quality, rigor and authenticity.

Rearrange Time

Most teachers agree that they are expected to waste huge amounts of time on unprofessional tasks. While there never seems to be enough time for study groups and professional development, they may be asked to stand guard duty and perform mindless tasks that can be reassigned. As mentioned earlier in this book, Carlene Murphy has reported dozens of practical strategies for teachers to find time to meet together in study groups in her 1997 **Staff Development Journal** article. http://www.nsdc.org/library/jsd/jsdsm97murp.html.

Shuffle Resources

Flexible and creative approaches to resources can free up surprising amounts of time and money to support new goals, but it takes an open mind and a willingness to challenge the way things are "spozed to be." Too much energy has gone into the cutting of worthwhile programs in order to fund hardware purchases.

Grants

There is a sudden emphasis upon professional development in most of the technology grant programs emerging from the U.S. Department of Education and many of the state departments. Enterprising districts can jump on this emergent trend and "make hay while the sun shines," but districts must always weigh the costs of grant writing against the odds of winning. They must also ask how they will maintain growth after the grant funding dries up. Grant Search Page http://www.tr.wou.edu/grant.htm

Picking Up the Tab

Bake Sales

In many schools, parent support for technology is a major technology funding source. Whether it be bake sales or art auctions, PTAs can sometimes generate thousands of dollars to support hardware purchase. Given the shortage of funds to support professional development, parents should be helped to see the importance of balance so they will devote a major share of their contributions to the human side of the equation.

Education Foundation

Some districts have been able to create a reliable and continuing stream of funding by establishing local foundations with the financial support of affluent citizens, alumni and local business interests. Many districts have only scratched the surface of this potential source. For more information on this strategy, consult the September, 1991 issue of **From Now On – The Educational Technology Journal.**
http://fno.org/fnosept91.html

Partners

Partnerships with technologically savvy local businesses can offer many adult learning opportunities in the form of visits, internships and the use of corporate resources and facilities. Many human resource managers are also good allies during the invention of adult learning programs.

References

ASLA and AECT. (1998) **Information Power: Building Partnerships for Learning.**

Deal, Terrence E. and Peterson, Kent D. (1998) **Shaping School Culture : The Heart of Leadership.** San Francisco: Jossey-Bass Publishers.

Eberle, Bob. (1997) **SCAMPER**. Prufrock Press.

Fullan, Micheal G. (1991) **The New Meaning of Educational Change**. New York: Teachers College Press.

Fullan, Micheal G.(1996) **What's Worth Fighting for in your School.** New York: Teachers College Press.

Joyce, Bruce R. and Weil, Marsha. (1996) **Models of Teaching.** Allyn & Bacon.

Joyce, B. (Ed). (1990) **Changing School Culture through Staff Development**. Alexandria, VA: ASCD.

Kelly, Kevin. (1998) **New Rules for the New Economy**. New York: Viking Penguin.

Lieberman, Ann and Miller, Lynne. (1999) **Teachers--Transforming Their World and Their Work**. New York: Teachers College Press.

Loucks-Horsley , Susan (Editor). (1997) **Designing Professional Development for Teachers of Science and Mathematics.** Newbury Park, California: Corwin Press.

McKenzie, Jamieson. (1993) **Power Learning**. Newbury Park, California: Corwin Press.

Moore, Geoffrey A. (1991) **Crossing the Chasm: Marketing and Selling High-Tech Products to Mainstream Customers**. New York: Harper Business.

Murphy, Carlene U.and Lick, Dale W. (1998) **Whole-Faculty Study Groups: A Powerful Way to Change Schools and Enhance Learning**. Newbury Park, CA: Corwin Press.

NCREL (North Central Regional Educational Lab). **Plugging In.**

Shenk, David. **(1997) Data Smog.** New York: Harper Edge.

Other Books and Videos
by Jamie McKenzie

Books

Beyond Technology: Questioning, Research and the Information Literate School (2000)

This book suggests ways to focus upon research and information literacy as the reason for networking schools. Suggests practical strategies to create stronger readers, writers and thinkers using the new technologies. Provides an emphasis upon standards-based learning. Available from FNO Press at http://fnopress.com

Planning Good Change with Technology and Literacy (2001)

Based on two decades of planning effectiveuses of new technologies, this book brings you thebest of Jamie McKenzie's thinking about launching successful technology programs with a major emphasis upon literacy and integrated learning. Available from FNO Press at http://fnopress.com

Administrators at Risk: Tools and Technologies to Secure Your Future (1993)

This book outlines the risks of maintaining "smokestack schools" and offers ways of leading schools towards a different kind of future which includes student-centered classrooms and an emphasis upon problem-solving. National Educational Service, 1252 Loesch Road, Bloomington, IN 47404-9107 phone (812) 336-7700 fax (812) 336-7790

Videos

Jamie McKenzie on the Internet:
A Tool for Research and Communication

Of all the exciting new technologies in today's classroom, perhaps no other has the potential to completely transform teaching and learning like the Internet. Dr. Jamie McKenzie offers practical ways to use the Internet to build learning skills and make classroom projects more meaningful. Authentic student presentations, teacher interviews, and online demonstrations illustrate practical applications of Internet projects.

Teachers will discover how to:

- Design Internet projects and identify online sources
- Enhance students' research, reading, and critical thinking skills
- Encourage student communication and collaboration
- Help students organize information
- Publish student work for a global audience.

Canter Associates, Inc.
Available from FNO Press at http://fnopress.com

How to Use the Internet in Your Classroom™
Canter Associates, Inc. January of 2000

What sets this course apart from other courses on the Internet?

- Emphasis upon information literacy and Information Power
- Focus on teachers learning by doing with Web activities
- Videos that show many rank and file teachers making effective use of these tools to support standards-based learning
- Activities to support staff study groups
- Many examples of scaffolded online research activities such as Research Modules, WebQuests and Telecollaborative Activities
- Leading Presenters: Bernie Dodge - Judy Harris - Jamie McKenzie

Canter Associates, Inc.
Available from FNO Press at http://fnopress.com

Index

A

B

C

Index

Index

Index

Guidance 17, 18, 23, 44, 47, 123
guide on the side 46, 47, 61

H

Hardware 4, 5, 9, 35, 66
Harmony 22, 119
Harris, Judi 26
Heroes 99, 109
High School 3, 25, 75, 76
hits 23, 44
Hodge podge 22
Hook 73, 130
Hype 17, 27

I

Imagebase 24
Incentives 132
Independence 12, 18, 19, 32, 57, 108, 109, 137, 151
Inertia 27
Inference 40, 68, 151
Inferential reasoning 41
Info-Glut 56, 57
Information 2, 3, 4, 5, 6, 7, 8, 9, 84, 85, 120, 122, 123, 125, 130, 141
Information Landscape 44
information landscape 23, 40, 42, 61, 68
Information literacy 11, 17, 59, 60, 62, 68, 141
information literacy 84
Information literate school community 59, 60, 62
Information Power 2, 7, 9
Infotective 40, 41, 49, 57
Infrastructure 4, 16, 35, 66, 124, 150
Insight 14, 21, 40, 41, 42, 43, 46, 48, 51, 52, 53, 55, 60, 61, 68
Integration 71, 89, 95, 97, 102, 123, 138, 139
Interpretation 13, 60, 61, 68
Interpretive 11
Intervention 29, 30, 31, 32
Inventive 17, 20, 21, 33, 35, 59, 117, 121, 131
Inventor 40, 72
Investigation 3, 16, 17, 42, 49, 69, 98
Investment 83, 84, 88
ISTE 85

Index

Index

Index

Index

Index

V

Virtual change 27, 115
Visual literacy 24

W

Web 8, 77, 84, 121, 123, 131, 138
WebQuest 17, 45, 101, 102, 105, 131, 153
Wired Classroom 46
Workplace Visit 93
Writing 3, 17, 22, 24, 28, 142